C

Adobe®
Acrobat® 7

Shari Nakano

Teach Yourself

Sams Publishing, 800 East 96th Street, Indianapolis, Indiana 46240 USA

Adobe® Acrobat® 7 in a Snap

Copyright © 2005 by Sams Publishing

International Standard Book Number: 0-672-32701-5

Library of Congress Catalog Card Number: 2004092817

Printed in the United States of America

First Printing: January 2005

08   07   06   05   4   3   2   1

Trademarks

Warning and Disclaimer

Bulk Sales

Sams Publishing offers excellent discounts on this book when ordered in quantity for bulk purchases or special sales. For more information, please contact

U.S. Corporate and Government Sales

1-800-382-3419

corpsales@pearsontechgroup.com

For sales outside the United States, please contact

International Sales

international@pearsoned.com

Acquisitions Editor
Betsy Brown

Development Editor
Jonathan A. Steever

Managing Editor
Charlotte Clapp

Project Editor
Matt Purcell

Production Editor
Megan Wade

Indexer
Erika Millen

Proofreader
Susan Eldridge

Technical Editor
Adam Pratt

Publishing Coordinator
Vanessa Evans

Interior Designer
Gary Adair

Page Layout
Susan Geiselman

About the Author

Shari Nakano is a web and graphics designer who has been in the computer industry for more than 10 years. She is currently the webmaster for a large agricultural firm near Santa Cruz, California, where she lives with her three cats, Kitty Bear, Sparky, and Dorian. When not working, she enjoys spending time with her family and getting together with friends for an evening of Texas hold 'em and computer games. She's currently taking a correspondence class on ice fishing.

Dedication

I would like to dedicate this book to my mother. Without her love and support, I wouldn't be where I am today. She's more than just my mom— she's my role model and inspiration. I can only hope to be more like her. I love you, Mom.

Acknowledgments

I would like to thank the great team of editors at Sams Publishing who have made writing this book a truly amazing experience for me: Matt Purcell, Jon Steever, Adam Pratt, Megan Wade, and Betsy Brown. Special thanks to Megan for her generous and helpful editorial contributions and to Betsy for her patience and guidance throughout the writing of this book.

This book would not have been possible without the help of Steve Samson. He was my mentor, my sounding board, and the one who talked me into taking that stupid ice fishing class. I would also like to thank Ted and Jennifer Alspach for all their help and support. Their knowledge of everything Adobe and Macintosh helped tremendously.

We Want to Hear from You!

As the reader of this book, *you* are our most important critic and commentator. We value your opinion and want to know what we're doing right, what we could do better, what areas you'd like to see us publish in, and any other words of wisdom you're willing to pass our way.

You can email or write me directly to let me know what you did or didn't like about this book—as well as what we can do to make our books stronger.

Please note that I cannot help you with technical problems related to the topic of this book, and that due to the high volume of mail I receive, I might not be able to reply to every message.

When you write, please be sure to include this book's title and author as well as your name and phone or email address. I will carefully review your comments and share them with the author and editors who worked on the book.

Email: consumer@samspublishing.com

Mail: Mark Taber
         Associate Publisher
         Sams Publishing
         800 East 96th Street
         Indianapolis, IN 46240 USA

Reader Services

For more information about this book or another Sams title, visit our website at www.samspublishing.com. Type the ISBN (excluding hyphens) or the title of a book in the Search field to find the page you're looking for.

PART I

Covering
the Basics

IN THIS PART:

1

✔ Start Here

Of the many software programs produced by Adobe Systems, Inc., Acrobat is the hardest one for most people to understand. Not that it's hard to learn—it's just hard to understand what you can use it for. Photoshop lets you retouch digital images, Illustrator lets you create logos and similar graphics, InDesign lets you lay out documents for publishing, GoLive lets you create websites, Premiere lets you edit video, and so on. But what does Acrobat do?

This chapter answers that question and gives you a brief introduction to this powerful software program. In this chapter you learn what Acrobat is and what it can do, as well as take a look at the interface and some basic tasks. The rest of the chapters dive deeper into the many features of Acrobat.

What Is Acrobat?

Adobe Acrobat and the Portable Document Format (*PDF*) file format that it uses have become the de facto standard for digital document distribution. There have been more than 500 million downloads of the free Adobe Reader software, which lets anyone in the world view and print the contents of PDF files. Because Acrobat is the software that is used to create those PDF files, it has also become enormously popular, beating out Adobe's powerhouse digital image-editing application Photoshop as Adobe's best-selling software program.

🔍 KEY TERM

PDF—Short for Portable Document Format, a cross-platform file format created by Adobe Systems for sharing files independently of the application that created the file or the operating system of either the file creator or the file viewer.

Adobe Acrobat and the PDF file format offer several significant features: platform-independent document distribution, unmatched document review and annotation, unmatched document security, online form creation and distribution, and online presentation capabilities.

Document Distribution

Cross-platform document distribution is the reason Acrobat and PDF came into existence. Before PDF, reading a document on a Macintosh that was created on a Windows computer (or vice versa) was an exercise in frustration. Even if both users had the same software application on each platform, and the software was supposed to be able to read files created in its sister application (and not all of them did), the fonts, layout, and images often didn't reproduce correctly.

Enter Adobe Acrobat and PDF documents. Suddenly, you could take a PDF document created on a Macintosh computer, view it on a Windows computer, print it on a Linux computer, and see the exact same output each time. Reliable cross-platform document distribution was finally here. And not only was PDF platform-independent, but it was also application-independent. It didn't matter if a document was originally created in Word or Excel or PageMaker or QuarkXpress; once it was converted to a PDF file, anyone could read it with the free Reader software. A designer with Illustrator and PageMaker on a Macintosh being able to create a file that could be viewed and approved by a client who had a Windows system with a suite of business applications was unheard of.

With the growth of the Internet, cross-platform document distribution became online document distribution, and the advantages of PDF made it the perfect file format for just about any file you would want to put on a website. The growth of the Internet turned Acrobat and PDF from a useful utility into the indispensable tool it is today.

Document Review

Another key feature of Acrobat and PDF is collaborative document review. This means a group of reviewers can add comments to a single document on a shared server or via a Web browser, or reviewers can add comments to their own copies of a document and then all the comments can be combined into a single, annotated PDF file.

Using Acrobat in the document review process lets you take advantage of the platform- and application-independent nature of PDF, as well as the wide variety of commenting tools Acrobat offers. For more information on reviewing documents with Acrobat, see **13** **About the Review Process** and **17** **Add Note Comments**.

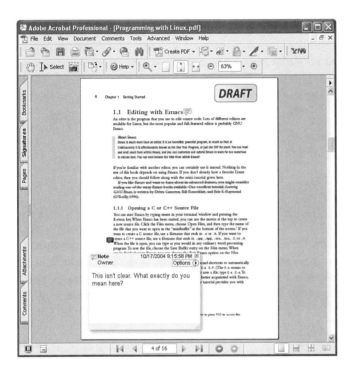

A PDF document with several types of comments.

Document Security

For anyone who works with sensitive data, Acrobat offers some very powerful document security features. Like many applications, Acrobat lets you password-protect documents. However, Acrobat's security is more far more powerful than the password protection offered by most business software programs. In addition to document-level password protection, Acrobat also lets you password-protect specific functionality within the document. You can easily create a document that anyone can view but that only people with the correct password can edit or print.

Acrobat also pioneered secure, digitally signed documents, which enable corporations all over the world to streamline their business operations without compromising the integrity of their documents and business

practices. With properly configured *digital signatures*, PDF forms, proposals, and other types of documents can be approved and processed online with a high level of confidence.

Online Forms

One of the truly great features of Acrobat is its capability to create online forms. Traditionally, computers didn't help much when it came to reducing the huge amount of day-to-day paperwork that was an inescapable part of doing business. Database programs still required someone to enter the information into the database from a printed form. This allowed a company to keep track of important information, but it didn't make the process any faster or easier.

PDF forms have all the advantages of regular PDF documents but also enable the user to enter data that can either be stored in the document itself or be uploaded to a website for automatic storage in a database. As Acrobat's form features have become better understood and more accessible to the business community, the use of PDF forms in the corporate world has grown by leaps and bounds. Expense reports, time sheets, requisitions, and purchase orders are just some of the everyday forms that can easily be replicated as PDF documents and completed, routed, and archived online.

Online Presentations

A final use for Acrobat is the creation and distribution of online or printed presentations. Acrobat isn't a presentation software program, but it does have a full-screen display mode complete with transition effects. This makes Acrobat or the free Adobe Reader software a perfect vehicle for distributing and delivering reliable, correctly formatted presentations. Because you can create PDFs from any application, you also have more flexibility in how you can choose to create the presentation in the first place. Presentations created in Illustrator or Photoshop can have a polish and sophistication (if you know what you are doing) that you simply can't achieve in a presentation software program. Of course, you can create a PDF from any application and add transition effects, video clips, sound effects and voiceovers, and onscreen buttons in Acrobat for a full-featured presentation with all the formatting reliability and distribution advantages of PDF. For more information on adding multimedia to a PDF, see **33 Create a Multimedia Link**.

The Acrobat Product Family

The Acrobat product family consists of several related products. These range from the free Adobe Reader software to the powerful, full-featured Professional version of Adobe Acrobat.

Reader

Most computer users are familiar with the free Adobe Reader software, formerly called Adobe Acrobat Reader. Unfortunately, many users have long been confused about the difference between Acrobat Reader and Acrobat itself, assuming that they had the full version of Acrobat on their computers just because they were able to view PDF files. This is one reason Adobe has renamed the Adobe Acrobat Reader to simply Adobe Reader. Another reason is that Reader lets you view or read more than just Acrobat PDF files. It also contains the functionality formerly found in Adobe eBook Reader, so Reader is now both a PDF and eBook viewing application. Adobe Reader 7.0 is available for free download from Adobe's website at www.adobe.com/reader. It can also be found on many software installation CDs because software manuals and read me files are often distributed in PDF format.

With the free Reader 7.0 software, you can

- View eBooks

- Open PDFs

- Print PDFs

- Complete and submit specially prepared PDF forms

- Add basic comments to specially prepared PDFs

Acrobat Standard

Acrobat Standard is the more basic of the two versions of Acrobat. It is intended for people who need to create and edit PDFs, but who don't need all the features of Acrobat Professional. The Standard version is a good solution for most individual and small business needs.

With Acrobat 7.0 Standard, you can

- Open PDFs

- Print PDFs

- Create, combine, and edit PDFs
- Add comments to PDFs

Acrobat Professional

KEY TERM

Preflighting—The process of checking a document for potential printing problems. It is most often used when preparing a document that will be sent to a commercial printing facility. Preflighting has traditionally required the use of third-party solutions.

Acrobat Professional is the most full-featured of all the Acrobat products. It is intended for commercial print shops, web and graphic designers, IT professionals, documentation specialists, and anyone else who needs full control over PDF creation and editing. The two main features of Acrobat Professional that the Standard version lacks are form creation and *pre-flighting*. Form creation is becoming an industry of its own, with PDF forms becoming more and more popular.

With Acrobat 7.0 Professional, you can

- Open PDFs
- Print PDFs
- Create, combine, and edit PDFs
- Add comments to PDFs
- Add form features to PDFs
- Work with layers
- Preflight documents for commercial output

Adobe Designer

One of the biggest new features of Acrobat 7.0 is the introduction of Adobe Designer. Adobe Designer is a standalone form creation application. For the first time ever, you can create your PDF forms from the ground up in a PDF environment. Previously, you had to create the layout of your form in a separate application, such as Illustrator or InDesign; convert the document to PDF; and then add form elements such as text field, check boxes, and drop-down lists in Acrobat.

Designer ships with Acrobat Professional, or it can be purchased separately. Designer is not currently available for Mac OS. If you are a Mac user, you have to create forms the old-fashioned way with Acrobat.

With Acrobat Designer 7.0, you can design PDF forms from scratch, from provided templates, or using a form design wizard.

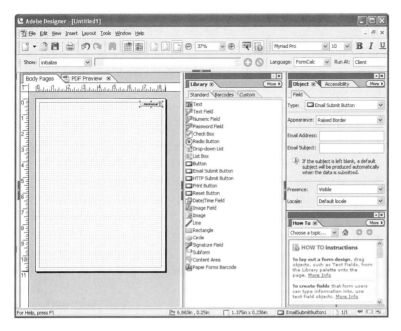

The Adobe Designer interface.

Acrobat Distiller

Even though Acrobat Distiller is not a "product" in the traditional sense (you cannot purchase it separately), it is a standalone application that is a critical part of Acrobat. It is installed automatically with both Acrobat Standard and Acrobat Professional. *Distiller* is the application that actually converts documents to the PDF format. Whether you print to PDF, use the PDFMaker buttons in Microsoft Office, or create a PDF from within Acrobat, the document data is sent to Distiller and Distiller creates the finished PDF version. Distiller runs in the background, out of sight, which is why most Acrobat users are unaware of Distiller's importance.

For the most part, you won't need to know much more than that about Distiller. Most documents convert to PDF using Distiller's standard settings with no problem. However, you can create better-quality output and smaller file sizes in certain circumstances by changing Distiller's conversion settings. See **77** **About Acrobat Distiller** for more information about working with Distiller.

KEY TERM

Distiller—It performs the actual converion of a document into a PDF file.

NOTE

One other product in the Acrobat family is Acrobat Elements. Acrobat Elements is a slightly less full-featured version of Acrobat Standard designed for large companies that want to standardize on PDF for their document distribution, review, and archival needs. It is available only as a large-scale enterprise solution, meaning it is not available for retail purchase to individuals.

New Features of Acrobat 7.0

The latest version of Acrobat, version 7.0, is a significant upgrade with a lot of enhancements and new features. The online help contains a comprehensive list of new features, so there is no need to list them all here, but here are our 10 favorite new features:

- **Acrobat Designer**—The ability to design and create a PDF form completely within an Acrobat product is a huge step forward and one the Acrobat community has been waiting for for a long time. Designer is included with Acrobat Professional or is available as a standalone product. It is currently available only for Windows.

- **Document review with Reader**—With Reader 7.0, document review is not limited only to those who own Acrobat itself. Reader 7.0 now has the capability to add comments to PDF files specially prepared with Acrobat 7 Professional.

- **Organizer**—Building on the popularity of Adobe's improved file management features in its graphic design products, Acrobat now sports a new Organizer feature that lets you easily locate and manage all the PDF files on your hard drive.

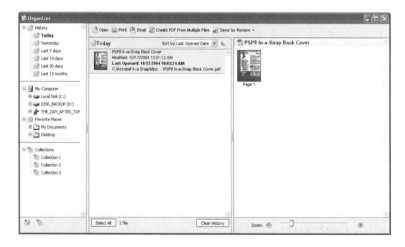

The Organizer window shows recent PDF documents.

- **Improved performance**—Adobe customers complained loud and long about Acrobat 6.0's startup times (especially on the Macintosh) and overall performance speed. Well, Adobe listened and Acrobat is noticeably faster overall and remarkably fast on startup.

- **Better headers and footers**—Headers and footers (as well as backgrounds and watermarks) are easier to create and modify, as well as printing more reliably, than in previous versions.

- **Technical tools and features**—Acrobat 7.0 makes it easier than ever for engineers and other technical professionals to create PDFs from their primary applications; it also offers measurement tools and technical commenting tools.

- **Attachments**—Attached files can be added more easily, as well as now being editable and searchable. Attached files are also automatically moved along with the PDF, and descriptions of each attached file appear in the new Attachment tab in the navigation pane.

- **Improved text comments**—You can now add text-based comments using a simple text-editing metaphor instead of having to enter and view all comments in pop-up windows. Text comments and edits can also be exported directly to the most recent versions of Microsoft Word on Windows.

- **Improved preflighting**—Acrobat's preflighting capabilities have been updated with enhanced output preview, password-protected profiles, printer marks, PDF/X compliance, and color separation previewing.

- **Improved accessibility**—The new Accessibility Setup Assistant makes it easier than ever to create documents for vision- and motion-impaired users. Preferences and shortcuts also make navigation easier for all users.

The Acrobat Interface

The Acrobat interface is divided into six separate areas: the toolbar well, document pane, navigation pane, comments pane, How To pane, and status bar. The toolbar well is always visible, and the document pane and status bar are visible whenever a document is open. The navigation pane, comments pane, and How To pane might not be visible at all times, but they are always available.

Navigation Pane

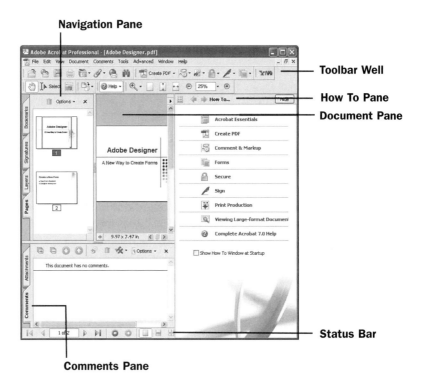

Toolbar Well

How To Pane

Document Pane

Status Bar

Comments Pane

The Acrobat interface.

Tools and Toolbars

Toolbar well—The area just under the menu bar where the Acrobat toolbars normally reside. You can drag toolbars out of the toolbar well to make them free-floating or drag them back to dock them with the other toolbars.

Acrobat has 15 toolbars, although only 6 of those are displayed for most documents. You can access all the toolbars through the **View** menu and **Toolbars** submenu. Selecting a toolbar in the **Toolbars** submenu displays it if it is not visible, or hides it if it is visible.

Toolbars are normally docked in the *toolbar well* just under the menu bar, but they can be moved to suit your needs. To move a toolbar, click the left edge of the toolbar and drag it to a new location. Once moved, you can dock a floating toolbar by dragging it back to the toolbar well.

Some tools are hidden beneath other tools. If additional tools are available beneath a tool, a small down arrow appears to the right of the tool, similar to the down arrow displayed to the right of most drop-down lists. For example, hidden beneath the **Zoom In** tool are the **Zoom Out**, **Dynamic Zoom**, and **Loupe** tools. To access a hidden tool, click the black arrow and select a new tool from those listed.

The Document Pane

The document pane is the main window in Acrobat. It displays your document, as well as a status bar at the bottom of the screen. The tools that let you control how your document is displayed are on the **Zoom** toolbar.

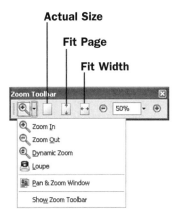

The Zoom toolbar.

The **Zoom** toolbar contains the **Zoom** tool, which can be used to zoom in or out of your document. To select this tool, click it in the toolbar and then click in your document to zoom in, or **Alt**-click (Windows) or **Option**-click (Mac OS) to zoom out. You can also click and drag in your document to zoom in to a specific location.

The **Zoom** toolbar also contains standard magnification controls that let you zoom in or out or enter a specific magnification percentage.

The three buttons on the **Zoom** toolbar you might not be familiar with are **Actual Size**, **Fit Page**, and **Fit Width**:

- **Actual Size**—Displays the page at 100% viewing size.

- **Fit Page**—Fits the entire page in the available document window space. This is good if you want to see what the page looks like but don't necessarily need to read the text on the page.

- **Fit Width**—Displays the document so you can see the entire width of the page; however, you need to scroll up and down to see the entire document. This is ideal if you want to be able to read the text on the page.

Acrobat's status bar, displayed at the bottom of the screen whenever you have a document open, doesn't present you with information like most status bars do. Instead, it provides additional controls for viewing your document.

Two buttons appear at the far left side of the status bar. The first button lets you view your document in full-screen (presentation) mode, and the second button hides your toolbars to provide more room for viewing your document. When the toolbars are hidden, a pop-up menu of basic tools and simple magnification controls are added to the status bar.

In the middle of the status bar are navigation controls that display the current page and contain buttons that take you to the first, previous, next, and last pages of the document, plus controls to go to the previous and next views. These controls are discussed in more detail in the **Viewing PDFs** section later in this chapter.

On the right side of the status bar are four layout buttons. These display your document in **Single Page** view, **Continuous** view, **Continuous Facing** view, and **Facing** view.

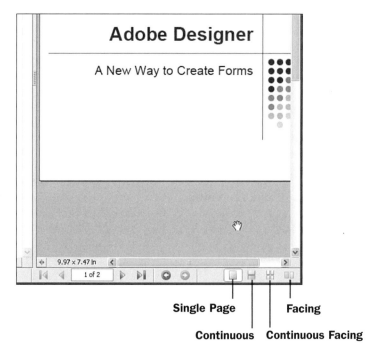

The document layout buttons.

The layout buttons do the following:

- **Single Page**—Displays the document one page at a time. When scrolling through the document, the current page is replaced by the next page.

- **Continuous**—Lets you smoothly scroll from the bottom of one page to the top of the next page, much like in a word processing application.

- **Continuous Facing**—Lets you smoothly scroll through your document but displays two pages at a time, as if you were looking at an open book.

- **Facing**—Displays two pages at a time but replaces the current two pages with the next two as you scroll through the document.

The Navigation Pane

Clicking the **Bookmarks**, **Signatures**, or **Pages** tab opens the navigation pane along the left side of the document pane. This pane displays the information about the bookmarks, digital signatures, or pages contained in the document.

The **Bookmarks**, **Signatures**, and **Pages** panels do the following:

- **Bookmarks**—Displays all prepared bookmarks for navigating within the document. See [42] **Create a Bookmark** for more information on using bookmarks.

- **Signatures**—Is empty if the document has not been digitally signed. If it has been signed, this panel displays information about the signatures and whether any changes have been made to the document since it was signed.

- **Pages**—Provides a quick way to navigate within the document by displaying thumbnails of each page. You can double-click the thumbnail of a particular page to go directly to that page in the document pane.

The Comments Pane

Clicking the **Comments** or **Attachments** tab opens the comments pane along the bottom of the document pane. This pane displays the contents of either the **Comments** or **Attachments** panel:

NOTE

Virtually all software applications refer to the interface elements you click to choose various sets of options within a dialog box as *tabs*. Adobe uses this term for the elements along the left side of the screen, which makes perfect sense. However, Adobe also refers to the information that appears after you click a tab as a *tab*. To avoid confusion, we use the term *panel* to refer to the information that is displayed. Instead of clicking a tab to open or close a tab, in this book we'll say something like "Click the **Bookmarks** tab to open or close the **Bookmark** panel."

The **Comments** and **Attachments** panels are used for the following:

- **Comments**—Lists all the comments that have been added to the document, along with a toolbar for managing those comments. See **13** **About the Review Process** and **24** **About the Comments Pane** for more information about comments.

- **Attachments**—Lists all the files that have been attached to the PDF file. A toolbar appears at the top of the **Attachments** panel with tools for opening, saving, adding, deleting, and searching attachments.

The How To Pane

The **How To** pane offers easy access to step-by-step instructions for common Acrobat tasks. By default, this pane opens when Acrobat launches, but many users turn off this behavior (by deselecting the **Show How To Window at Startup** check box) so they have more screen real estate available for their documents.

Using the **How To** pane is like using the easiest website imaginable. At the top of the pane are **Home**, **Previous**, and **Next** buttons, as well as a button to hide the pane altogether. The rest of the pane consists of a list of topics, each of which is a clickable link that displays related tasks. Each of these tasks is a clickable link that displays a page of instructions on how to perform that task, as well as hyperlinks for related topics.

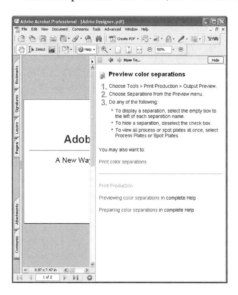

*The **How To** pane displays simple help text.*

Viewing PDFs

The key function of Adobe Reader, and still one of the key functions of Adobe Acrobat, is opening and viewing PDF files. This section discusses some of the basics of viewing PDFs.

When you open a PDF document, it is usually displayed in **Fit Page** mode, letting you see the entire contents of the first page of the document in the document pane. For easier reading, you can click the **Actual Size** or **Fit Width** button in the **Zoom** toolbar, as discussed earlier in this chapter in the section **The Document Pane**.

Moving from one page to another can be done in several ways, depending on whether you prefer to use the mouse or keyboard. With the mouse, you can scroll down with the mouse wheel (Windows) or with the document pane scrollbars, or you can click the page navigation buttons in the middle of the status bar. These buttons let you go to the first page of the document, the previous page, the next page, or the last page. You can also click in the text field that displays the current page number, type a new page number, and press the **Enter** key to jump directly to that page. If you prefer to navigate with the keyboard, the **Home**, **Page Up**, **Page Down**, and **End** keys take you to the first, previous, next, and last pages of the document, respectively.

Also on the status bar are the **Previous View** and **Next View** buttons. These function just like the **Back** and **Next** buttons on a web browser, but for *views*, instead of pages. A view is anything that is displayed in the document pane and includes the document, page, location, and magnification level. The **Previous View** button takes you back to the last portion of this document or another document you viewed; after you have used the **Previous View** button, the **Next View** button lets you move forward again through your views.

One other handy navigation technique is the **Hand**, or **Browse**, tool (the default tool in Acrobat). Clicking in the document pane and moving the mouse lets you move your document within the document pane. Although this is not a very efficient way to move from page to page, it is a quick and easy way to move within a page, especially if you have zoomed in to view a relatively small portion of a page.

NOTE

If a document doesn't open in **Fit Page** mode, it means either you have changed your preferred display mode through the **Edit**, **Preferences** command or the author of the PDF has changed the document's initial view through the **File**, **Document Properties** command. If an initial view isn't set for a document by its author, it always opens according to the application preferences of the viewer.

KEY TERM

View—The visible contents of the document pane. Views include the document, page, page location, and magnification level.

2

Creating a PDF

IN THIS CHAPTER:

KEY TERM

Portable Document Format (PDF)—A widely used file format that preserves the font, image, and formatting integrity of the original source document and makes it viewable across almost any operating system.

Portable Document Format (PDF) was created by Adobe Systems to establish a universal file format that is accessible by anyone on any computer running almost any operating system in the world (as long as the free Adobe Reader program is installed, which is available to download at http://www.adobe.com/reader). In addition to this universal accessibility, the two other primary reasons to create a PDF version of a document is that the PDF format preserves both the appearance and formatting integrity of the original source document.

Acrobat can convert just about any document to the PDF format. This includes scanned documents or images; files created with other Adobe products such as InDesign, Illustrator, GoLive, and Photoshop; Microsoft Word, Excel, PowerPoint, Publisher, and Outlook files; web pages; AutoCAD files; and more. The following list includes file formats supported by Acrobat:

- AutoDesk AutoCAD
- AutoDesk Inventor
- BMP
- CompuServe GIF
- HTML
- JDF Job Definition
- JPEG
- JPEG2000
- Microsoft Access
- Microsoft Office
- Microsoft Publisher
- Microsoft Visio
- PCX
- PDF
- PNG
- PostScript/EPS
- Text
- TIFF
- XML

Even though many people (including us) refer to Acrobat's ability to "create PDFs," it is important to keep in mind that Acrobat doesn't really create anything. It converts existing documents to the PDF file format and then lets you do some pretty amazing things with that PDF file, but you must use some other application to actually create the source document. If you look at Acrobat's toolbars and menus, you won't see a **New** command as in most other applications.

Acrobat offers several ways to convert a file to the PDF format, ranging from creating a PDF from single and multiple files, to creating a PDF version of an entire website to creating PDFs in other applications.

Create a PDF in Acrobat

Converting a document to PDF format is a remarkably simple process. Basically, you just point Acrobat to a *source document* and let Acrobat take it from there. Of course, there is a bit more to it than that. Depending on the operating system and document type being used, Acrobat might launch the application that created the source file and use that application to print the document to Adobe Distiller, which is where the actual conversion to PDF takes place. In other cases, Acrobat simply performs the PDF conversion itself and displays the file. And there are a few things you can do after the PDF has been created to customize how it is viewed.

1 Choose the Source Document

From the **File** Menu, select **Create PDF, From File**. In the **Open** dialog box that appears, locate and open the document you want to convert to PDF. A series of information screens and progress bars let you know what is going on during the conversion process.

2 View the PDF

Press the **Page Down** key or click the **Next Page** button located at the bottom of the document window to view your new PDF document.

See Also

→ **6** Insert Pages
→ **26** Secure a PDF File with Password Protection

 TIPS

Clicking the **Create PDF** button on the **Task** toolbar brings up the same submenu options as does selecting **Create PDF** from the **File** menu.

Acrobat does an excellent job converting a remarkable range of file types to PDF. However, you can customize the conversion settings for any specific file type by going to the **Edit** menu and selecting the **Preferences** command. In the **Preferences** dialog box, click **Convert to PDF**, select the desired file format, and click the **Edit Settings** button. The parameters you can adjust vary from one file type to another. Most graphical file formats let you modify color and compression settings, whereas most document file formats allow you to choose from predefined document conversion and security settings. For more information on customizing conversion settings, see **80** **Create Custom Settings**.

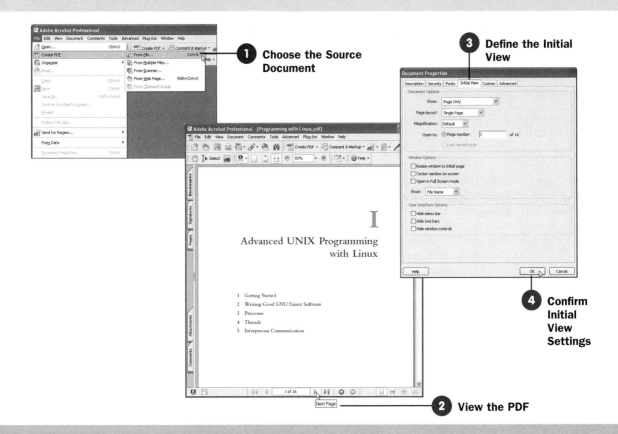

1 Choose the Source Document

3 Define the Initial View

4 Confirm Initial View Settings

2 View the PDF

3 Define the Initial View

After you have created the PDF, you might want to specify how the file should be displayed when it is first opened. By default, only the document pane appears and it uses whatever magnification and layout settings the person viewing the file has set in his Acrobat preferences.

To set the opening view for your PDF, click the **File** menu and select the **Document Properties** command. The **Document Properties** dialog box opens. Click the **Initial View** tab to display document, window, and user interface options.

The **Document Options** section contains drop-down lists where you can choose whether you want the document to open with just the document pages displayed or with document pages plus the

Bookmarks, Pages, Attachments, or Layers panels open as well. You can also choose the page layout, magnification level, and which page is initially displayed.

The **Window Options** section contains controls that are used far less often but are still occasionally useful. They include check boxes to resize the document window to fit the initial page, to center the window on the screen, to open the file in full-screen mode (like a PowerPoint slideshow), and a choice between displaying the filename or document title (set in the **Description** tab of the **Document Properties** dialog box) in the title bar.

Finally, the **User Interface Options** section lets you hide the menu bar, toolbars, and window controls when the file is opened. This is generally not recommended unless you have a *very* good reason for not wanting to allow the viewer access to these critical interface elements. About the only circumstance in which this is acceptable would be for a self-running presentation on a public-access computer, such as at a trade show or other event kiosk.

4 Confirm Initial View Settings

Click the **OK** button to apply your settings to your new PDF file. To test the initial view options, save, close, and reopen the file.

2 Create a PDF from Multiple Files

Whether it's a matter of consolidating monthly reports, creating a log of emails, or pulling together disparate parts of a presentation, there will be plenty of times when you will want to create a single PDF file from multiple source documents. Acrobat makes creating multisource PDF files from either raw source documents or from existing PDFs easy.

1 Choose Source Documents

From the **File** menu, select **Create PDF**, **From Multiple Files**. In the **Create PDF from Multiple Documents** dialog box, click the **Browse** (Windows) or **Add** (Mac OS) button and locate and add files to the **Files to Combine** list. Both existing PDFs and files still in their original file formats can be combined together. Acrobat automatically converts non-PDFs when combining them.

NOTE

Document templates are a new addition to Acrobat 7. They are basically blank PDF forms you can use as the basis for new PDF documents. The new templates include a Memo template, an Envelopes template, and a From File template that allows you to create a new PDF document based on an existing PDF form.

Before You Begin

✔ **1** Create a PDF in Acrobat

See Also

→ **6** Insert Pages

→ **7** Extract Pages

→ **26** Secure a PDF File with Password Protection

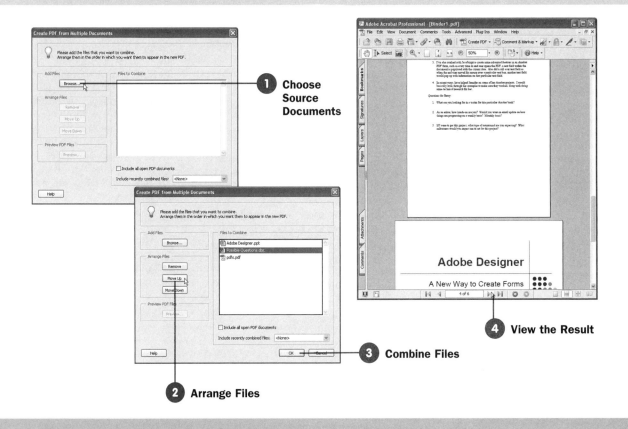

1 Choose Source Documents

2 Arrange Files

3 Combine Files

4 View the Result

TIP

A **Create PDF from Multiple Files** button appears in the **Organizer** that is identical in effect to the **From Multiple Files** command in the **Create PDF** submenu. They both bring up the **Create PDF from Multiple Documents** dialog box. The advantage of doing this from inside the **Organizer** is that, if you are combining multiple PDFs, locating them in the **Organizer** can be easier than in a standard **Open** dialog box.

To automatically have all open PDFs added to the list, click the **Include All Open PDF Documents** check box at the bottom of the **Files to Combine** list. You can also select recently combined files from the **Include Recently Combined Files** drop-down list; all files used in that recently combined file are then added to the **Files to Combine** list.

2 Arrange Files

Arrange the files in the order in which you want them to be added to the PDF by clicking the file to move and then clicking either the **Move Up** or **Move Down** button. You can also move a file up or down by selecting the file and, while holding down with the left mouse button, dragging it up or down and dropping it at the desired location. If you've added a file by mistake, just select that file and click the **Remove** button.

3 Combine Files

Click the **OK** button at the bottom of the **Create PDF from Multiple Documents** dialog box, and then sit back and relax as Acrobat combines all the listed files into a single PDF. This process can take a minute or two as Acrobat opens the different source applications and converts all the source documents.

4 View the Result

When the process is complete, press the **Page Down** key or click the **Next Page** button at the bottom of the document window to view the newly combined files.

3 Convert a Website to a PDF

One very cool feature of Acrobat is its capability to create PDFs out of entire websites for archival purposes or for viewing at a time when you might not have Internet access (such as on a long airplane flight). Acrobat does a good job of capturing the information in the website, although it doesn't always get the formatting right.

See Also

→ **46** Organize Bookmarks

1 Specify a URL

From the **File** menu, select **Create PDF**, **From Web Page**. In the **Create PDF from Web Page** dialog box, enter the URL of the web page you want to convert. Or, you can click the **Browse** button and navigate to a previously saved web page on your computer.

2 Select Settings

In the **Settings** section, choose how many levels deep into the website you want Acrobat to go to retrieve pages. Choosing 1 level downloads only the specified URL. Choosing 2 levels downloads the specified URL plus any pages you can link to from the specified URL. Obviously, the deeper into the website you go, the bigger the resulting PDF will be. If you choose to download the entire site, Acrobat warns you it might take a long time and also create a very large file.

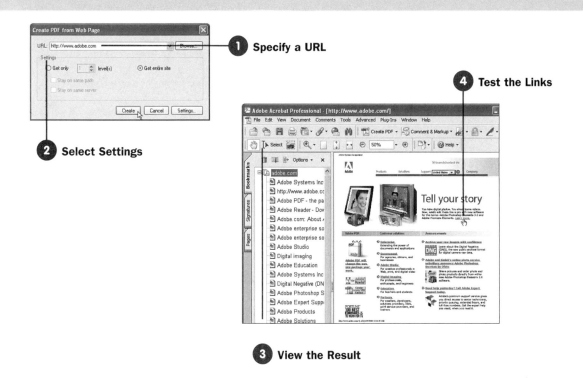

1 Specify a URL

4 Test the Links

2 Select Settings

3 View the Result

TIP

Acrobat asks how you want to view linked web pages (in your browser or downloaded into a PDF file) only the first time you click a link in a PDF, but you can access it at any time by going to the **Edit** menu, selecting the **Preferences** command, clicking **Web Capture** in the **Categories** list, and selecting either **In Acrobat** or **In Web Browser** from the **Open in** drop-down list. Whichever way you set Acrobat to open web links, you can toggle how a link is opened by holding down the **Shift** key as you click it.

3 View the Result

Click the **Create** button and Acrobat converts the web page(s) to a PDF. Depending on the complexity of the web page (especially if frames are used), the PDF version will probably not exactly match the web version. However, the bulk of the text and graphics should display correctly and the links should all work as intended. Acrobat creates bookmarks of all the pages (see **42** **Create a Bookmark**, for details on working with bookmarks), which you can click to jump to a specific web page.

4 Test the Links

You can also click any link on any of the web pages. If the page has not already been downloaded into the PDF, Acrobat prompts you to choose between downloading the link and viewing it in Acrobat or launching your web browser and viewing it there.

4 Create PDFs from Microsoft Office

You can create a PDF document directly from a number of Microsoft Office applications, such as Word and PowerPoint. In fact, you don't even have to exit an Office product to create a PDF. If Microsoft Office is installed on your computer when you install Acrobat, the Acrobat installer adds a set of macros (collectively referred to as PDFMaker) and a new toolbar to your Office applications. The net result is that three new buttons (**Convert to Adobe PDF**, **Convert to Adobe PDF and Email**, and **Convert to Adobe PDF and Send for Review**) in your Office toolbar area and a new menu (**Adobe PDF**) in the menu bar. The **Adobe PDF** menu contains three commands that correspond to the three new toolbar buttons, as well as a command to change PDF conversion settings.

1 Open the Source Document

Open a document in Microsoft Word. The settings for all Office products are similar, but Microsoft Word has the most options, so step 2 assumes you have opened a Word document. If you are converting an Excel or a PowerPoint document, you can ignore the explanations of the **Word** and **Bookmarks** tabs.

2 Select Conversion Settings

From the **Adobe PDF** menu, select **Change Conversion Settings**. In the **Acrobat PDFMaker** dialog box are four tabs from which to choose: **Settings**, **Security**, **Word**, and **Bookmarks**.

The **Settings** tab allows you to change the PDFMaker settings before converting a document. The **Conversion Settings** drop-down list lets you choose from a variety of default conversion settings. Of the available settings, most users stick with **Standard**, although you might want to use **High Quality** or **Press Quality** for PDFs that will be output to high-end printers or **Smallest File Size** for documents that will be viewed only online. There are also check boxes you can deselect if you do not want to view the finished PDF, set a name and location for the PDF, or transfer Word document information to the PDF version of the document.

Before You Begin

✔ **1** Create a PDF in Acrobat

See Also

→ **6** Insert Pages
→ **7** Extract Pages
→ **26** Secure a PDF File with Password Protection
→ **42** Create a Bookmark
→ **45** Generate Bookmarks from Structured Documents

 NOTE

If your Microsoft Office products were installed after Acrobat, the Adobe PDF buttons and menu do not appear in your Microsoft Office products. However, you can add them with a few easy steps. Just launch Acrobat, click the **Help** menu, and select the **Detect and Repair** command. This launches the Acrobat installer, reinstalls any damaged or missing functionality in Acrobat or supported source applications, such as Microsoft Office products.

 NOTE

When converting a document to PDF, the file is automatically saved to the same folder as the source file. The PDF is saved with the same name as the source file, but with the **.pdf** extension.

1 **Open the Source Document**

2 **Select Conversion Settings**

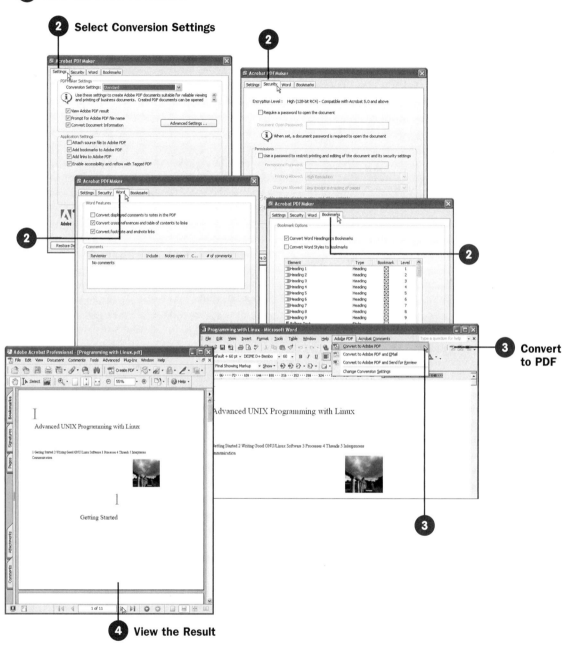

3 **Convert to PDF**

4 **View the Result**

The **Security** tab allows you to set a password to restrict opening, printing, or editing the document. It gives you the same options available when setting document security in Acrobat. See **26** **Secure a PDF File with Password Protection** for details.

The **Word** tab has features that enable you to choose to convert comments to notes, convert cross-references and table of contents to links, and convert footnotes and endnotes. Also on the Word tab is a **Comments** box that displays comments on the document.

On the **Bookmark** tab, you can choose which Word *styles* you want converted to Acrobat Bookmarks. Obviously, this is useful only if you have conscientiously applied styles throughout your document. But if you have, it's amazingly handy to have your newly generated PDF file already populated with bookmarks.

3 Convert to PDF

From the **Adobe PDF** menu, select **Convert to Adobe PDF** or click the **Convert to Adobe PDF** button in the toolbar. The PDFMaker macros start and the document is converted to PDF format. Toward the end of the process you are presented with a standard **Save** dialog box in which you can enter a name and specify a different location for your new PDF.

4 View the Result

When the PDF is created and automatically opened for viewing, press the **Page Down** key or click the **Next Page** button at the bottom of the document window to view the newly combined files.

KEY TERM

Style—A set of formatting instructions that can be quickly applied to selected text. Styles are a common feature in word processing and page layout applications.

NOTE

The **Create Adobe PDF** button and command creates a PDF of the default view for your document. If you want any view but the default (such as Word's outline mode and PowerPoint outline, notes pages, or handouts), you will not be able to use the PDFMaker macros. Instead, you need to print the document to the Adobe PDF printer driver as described in **5** **About Creating a PDF from Other Applications**.

 About Creating a PDF from Other Applications

You can create PDFs from virtually any software application. As long as you have Acrobat installed on your computer and the application from which you want to create a PDF has a **Print** command, you can create a PDF from that application.

You can also create PDFs using the **Export** or **Save As** command in many applications, especially image editing and page layout applications. For example, Adobe InDesign has an **Export** command specifically designed to let you output PDF versions of your page layout documents with a wide variety of custom PDF options. Adobe Illustrator makes it even easier, allowing you to select PDF as one of the file format options in its **Save As** dialog box.

Regardless of whether an application supports direct export/save in PDF format, you can always print the file to PDF by selecting the **Print** command in whatever application you are working in, changing the printer to Adobe PDF in the drop-down printer selection list, and then clicking the **Print** button. Your application sends the document data to Adobe Acrobat Distiller instead of to a printer, and Distiller creates a PDF version of the file and prompts you for a name and a location in which to save it. For more information about Distiller and how it differs from Acrobat itself, see **77** About Acrobat Distiller.

3

Modifying a PDF File

IN THIS CHAPTER:

NOTE

New to Acrobat 7: The **Pages**, **Set Page Transitions**, **Insert Pages**, **Extract Pages**, **Replace Pages**, **Delete Pages**, **Crop Pages**, and **Rotate Pages** commands are located in the main **Documents** menu, rather than being contained in a separate **Pages** submenu as they were in Acrobat 6.

Besides enabling you to convert documents to PDF format, Acrobat also enables you to make changes to the PDF, such as inserting, deleting, moving, cropping pages, renumbering pages, adding headers and footers, and making minor modifications to text. In general, combining and modifying pages can be done in Acrobat, but any major content changes—such as significant text edits or major modifications to the page layout—should always be done in the original authoring application and to the original source documents.

6 Insert Pages

Before You Begin

✔ **1** Create a PDF in Acrobat

See Also

→ **10** Renumber Pages

KEY TERM

Cropping—The process of trimming away unwanted areas around the perimeter of a page or a selected portion of a page.

It is not at all uncommon for a PDF file to consist of pages from several different source documents. For example, you may need to create a PDF report that contains two different Word documents, an Excel spreadsheet and multiple design documents created in Illustrator or Photoshop. Acrobat allows you to insert pages from as many different documents as you like into a single PDF file. However, Acrobat will only let you insert pages from other PDF files, so you will need to convert all of your source documents into PDFs before you start inserting pages. Also, the Insert Pages command inserts all pages from the source file. You will then need to delete any unwanted pages, as well as moving, rotating or *cropping* pages as needed.

When working with pages, it is helpful to open the Pages panel of the navigation pane by clicking on the **Pages** tab on the left side of the document window. The Pages panel displays small thumbnail versions of every page in the document. Clicking on any page in the **Pages** panel displays that page in the document pane.

Choose a Source Document

From the **Document** menu, select the **Insert Pages** command. In the **Select File to Insert** dialog box, locate and open the PDF file that contains the pages you want to insert.

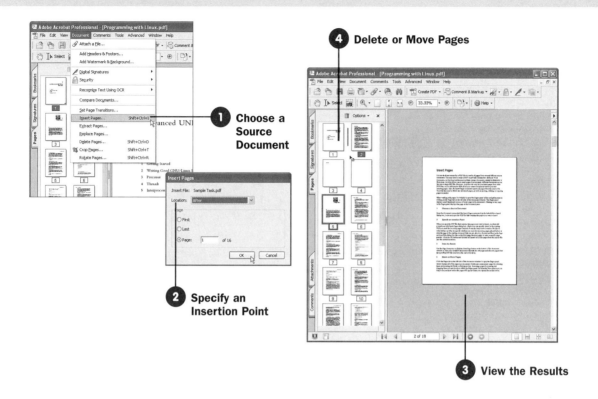

4 Delete or Move Pages

1 Choose a Source Document

2 Specify an Insertion Point

3 View the Results

2 Specify an Insertion Point

When you open the PDF file that contains the pages you want to insert, Acrobat presents the **Insert Pages** dialog box, where you can specify where in the existing PDF you want the incoming pages inserted. From the drop-down **Location** list, select either **Before** or **After** (to specify whether you want the incoming pages placed before or after the page in the existing document that you are about to choose); then in the **Page** section of the dialog box, select **First Page** or **Last Page**, or enter a specific page number. Click the **OK** button and Acrobat inserts all the pages from the source file into the current document at the location you specified.

Insert Pages

TIP

If you have two PDF files open simultaneously, you can insert just the pages you want by dragging them from one document to the other. First, tile the two document windows by clicking the **Window** menu, selecting **Tile**, and selecting either **Vertically** or **Horizontally**. Open the **Pages** panel in each window by clicking the **Pages** tab in the **Navigation** pane of each window, and then simply drag the desired pages from the **Pages** panel of the source file to the **Pages** panel of the destination file. To move multiple pages from one **Pages** panel to the other, hold down the **Ctrl** key and click the thumbnails of the pages to be moved. Release the **Ctrl** key and then drag the pages to the **Pages** panel of the destination file.

③ View the Results

Press the **Page Down** key or click the **Next Page** button at the bottom of the document window to view your modified document with both the old pages and the new pages from the specified PDF file inserted in the correct location.

④ Delete or Move Pages

Click the **Pages** tab on the left side of the document window to open the **Pages** panel, which displays all the pages in a document. Delete any unnecessary pages by selecting them and pressing the **Delete** or **Backspace** key. Rearrange pages by clicking and dragging them to a new location within the **Pages** panel. An insertion line appears as you drag to let you know where the pages will appear when you release the mouse button.

⑦ Extract Pages

See Also

→ ② Create a PDF from Multiple Files

→ ⑩ Renumber Pages

KEY TERM

Extracting—Extracting a page or range of pages creates a new PDF file that contains those pages. The selected page or pages can be deleted from the original document, if desired, during the process.

Just as you might occasionally need to combine pages from multiple PDFs into a single file, you might also need to sometimes *extract* pages from a PDF into a separate file. Extracting pages creates one or more separate files from individual pages or a range of pages within a PDF.

① Specify Pages to Be Extracted

From the **Document** menu, select the **Extract Pages** command. At the top of the **Extract Pages** dialog box, specify the page range you want extracted from the current document.

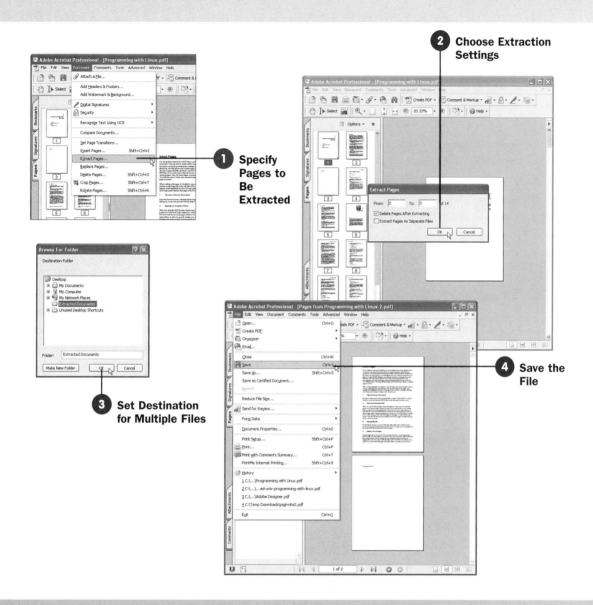

2 Choose Extraction Settings

1 Specify Pages to Be Extracted

3 Set Destination for Multiple Files

4 Save the File

---

2 **Choose Extraction Settings**

Click the **Delete Pages After Extracting** check box if you want the page range you specified in step 1 to be deleted from your document. If you leave this check box unselected, your current document will be unaffected by the extraction.

Click the **Extract Pages As Separate Files** check box if you want each page in the extraction range to be saved as a separate, one-page PDF file. If you leave this check box unselected, all the pages will be extracted into a single PDF file.

After you have made your extraction choices, click the **OK** button. Acrobat then extracts the pages.

3 **Set Destination for Multiple Files**

If you selected the **Extract Pages As Separate Files** check box in step 2, Acrobat presents a **Browse for Folder** dialog box. When this dialog box appears, either navigate to the folder where you want the single-page PDF files to be saved or click the **Make New Folder** button and create a new folder. When a location has been selected or created, click the **OK** button and Acrobat saves all the extracted pages as individual files in the specified location. The name of each file is the name of the original PDF document plus the page number (for example, pages 18–20 of the Annual Report would be saved as **Annual Report 18**, **Annual Report 19**, and **Annual Report 20**).

4 **Save the File**

If you did not select the **Extract Pages As Separate Files** check box in step 2, Acrobat extracts the specified pages into a new file named **Pages from** plus the name of the original file. This is a temporary name only; Acrobat prompts you to save the file before closing it or exiting Acrobat.

---

8 **Crop Pages**

Before You Begin

✔  Create a PDF in Acrobat

✔  Create a PDF from Multiple Files

See Also

→ **9** Rotate Pages

→ **38** View a PDF in Full Screen View

Cropping refers to setting display or print boundaries that are smaller than the original document dimensions. Acrobat allows you to crop several different types of document margins for screen display, printing, high-end printing, and print production.

Cropping only defines what portion of the document is displayed or printed, it does not actual alter the information in the document in any way.

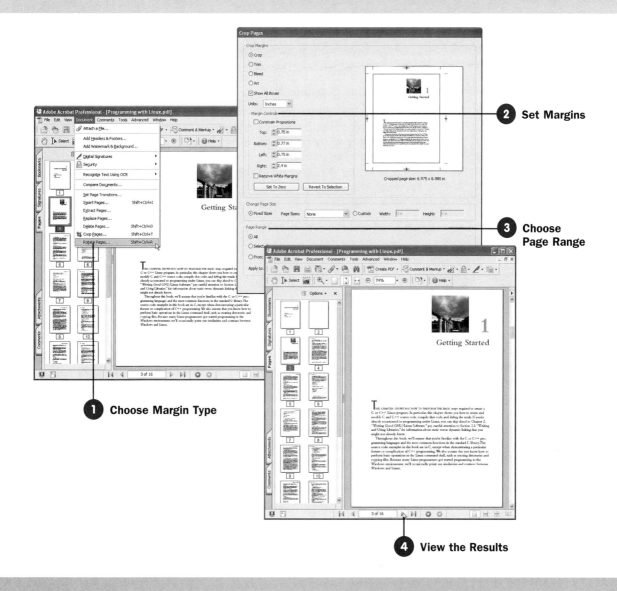

2 Set Margins

3 Choose Page Range

1 Choose Margin Type

4 View the Results

1 Choose Margin Type

From the **Document** menu, select the **Crop Pages** command. In the **Crop Pages** dialog box, select which type of margin you want to work with:

- **Crop**—The default option, it defines the area of the document that will be displayed or printed.

- **Trim**—Defines what the document will look like after it has been professionally printed and trimmed, folded, or otherwise prepared.

- **Bleed**—Defines the area of the document that will be printed if the printing is done at a professional print facility. The *bleed* is the area of a document outside the intended final dimensions.

- **Art**—Defines the boundary of the page, including white space.

You can also select the **Show All Boxes** check box if you want to see indicators for all four margins in the preview, or you can leave it unchecked to see only the margin you are working with.

② Set Margins

After you have selected your margin type, either click the up and down arrows or type in values for the **Top**, **Bottom**, **Left**, and **Right** margins. The margin indicators in the preview move to show you how the different values will affect your document.

If you want to use identical values for all four margins, select the **Constrain Proportions** check box. To reset all values to 0, click the **Set to Zero** button.

③ Choose Page Range

In the **Page Range** section of the **Crop Pages** dialog box, specify which pages you want to affect. You can choose from three options when selecting a page range. You can select **All** pages to crop, just the **Selected** page (the page currently active in the document window), or a specific **Page Range**. After selecting the page range, click **OK** to accept the new values.

④ View the Results

Use the **Page Down** key or click the **Next Page** button at the bottom of the document window to view your modified document. If you are not happy with the result, simply return to the **Document** menu, select the **Crop Pages** command again, and either change the margins or set them back to zero.

TIP

Acrobat offers two ways to set cropping dimensions: The margin controls in the **Crop Pages** dialog box or the **Crop** tool. To select the **Crop** tool, go to the **Advanced Editing** submenu found under **Tools**. Using the **Crop** tool enables you to manually set the cropping dimensions by dragging a rectangle around a portion of the page. After you have defined the cropping dimensions, press the **Enter** key to open the **Crop Pages** dialog box and finish the process.

9 Rotate Pages

When working with a PDF file created from a single source document, you probably won't have to rotate any pages. However, if you create PDFs from multiple files or insert pages into a PDF, you might need to rotate some of the pages so they all have the same orientation. For example, if you combine PowerPoint slides and an Excel spreadsheet with a Word document, you might want to rotate the slides and the spreadsheet so all the pages in the PDF have a portrait orientation.

1 Select Pages

Click the **Pages** tab on the left side of the document window to open the **Pages** panel. Select the pages you want to rotate by clicking a single page and then Shift-clicking or Ctrl-clicking (⌘-clicking on Mac OS) any additional pages you want to select.

If you want to rotate all pages or a contiguous range of pages, you can skip this step and specify the desired pages in step 3.

2 Choose a Direction

From the **Document** menu, select the **Rotate Pages** command. In the **Rotate Pages** dialog box, select **Clockwise 90 Degrees**, **Counterclockwise 90 Degrees**, or **180 Degrees** from the **Direction** drop-down list.

3 Choose Page Range

If you selected pages in the **Pages** panel in step 1, click the **Selection** option in the **Page Range** section of the **Rotate Pages** dialog box. If not, either click **All** or click **Pages** and enter the first and last pages of the desired page range.

In the first **Rotate** drop-down list, select whether you want to rotate **Even and Odd Pages**, **Even Pages Only**, or **Odd Pages Only**. (Because of the way a book is bound, odd pages always appear on the right side of an open book and even pages always appear on the left side.)

In the second **Rotate** drop-down list, select whether you want to rotate **Pages of Any Orientation**, **Landscape Pages** (pages that are wider than they are tall), or **Portrait Pages** (pages that are taller than they are wide).

Before You Begin

✔ **6** Insert Pages

See Also

→ **8** Crop Pages
→ **38** View a PDF in Full Screen View

 TIP

To temporarily rotate the view of a page, go to the **View** menu and select **Rotate View** and then either **Clockwise** or **Counterclockwise** from the submenu. Rotated views do not affect the document itself, only the way it is displayed for the current viewing session. Rotated views cannot be saved.

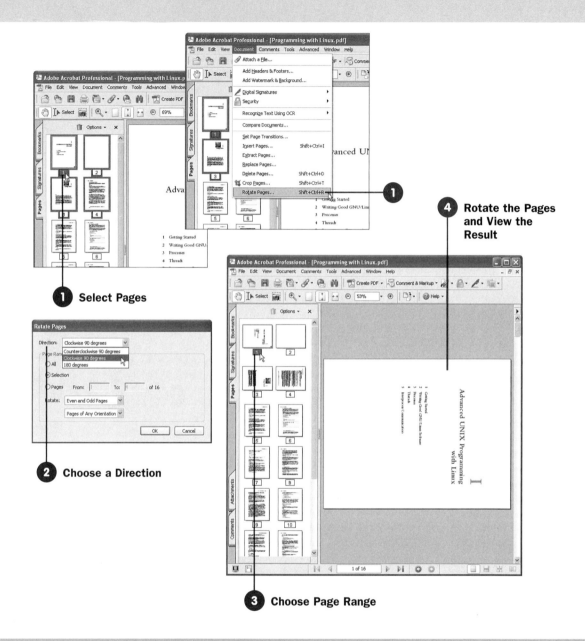

1 Select Pages

2 Choose a Direction

3 Choose Page Range

4 Rotate the Pages and View the Result

4 Rotate the Pages and View the Result

After you have set all your options, click the **OK** button at the bottom of the **Rotate Pages** dialog box. Acrobat then rotates the specified pages based on those options. The rotated pages are now displayed both in the **Pages** panel and the document window.

10 Renumber Pages

At the bottom of the document window are the page navigation controls. These controls include buttons to go from one page to another, as well as an indicator that shows the page you are currently viewing. The page numbers shown here refer to the actual page in the PDF document, which might not have any page numbers that were created for the document in the original authoring application. This is especially true of documents with front matter, such as a table of contents, copyright page, dedication, and so on. If the page number displayed by Acrobat does not match the internal document page numbers, it can cause confusion, especially when trying to refer to a particular page in discussions with other viewers of the PDF.

Acrobat lets you renumber as many different page ranges as necessary, as well as using different numbering styles, such as lowercase Roman numbering for front matter.

1 Specify Page Range

Click the **Pages** tab on the left side of the document window to open the **Pages** panel. Click the **Options** menu at the top of the **Pages** panel and select **Number Pages**. This brings up the **Page Numbering** dialog box.

At the top of the dialog box, select either **All** or **Selected** (if you have a range of pages selected in the **Pages** panel). Or you can specify a range of pages in the **From** and **To** boxes.

2 Choose Numbering Options

In the **Numbering** area of the **Page Numbering** dialog box, choose either **Begin New Section** or **Extend Numbering Used in Preceding Section to Selected Pages**. If you choose to begin a new section, select a numbering style (such as **1**, **2**, **3**; **A**, **B**, **C**; or **i**, **ii**, **iii**) from the **Style** drop-down list. You can also specify a prefix for the page numbers (to have a section numbered Intro-1, Intro-2, Intro-3, and so on, for example) and at which number you want the page numbering to start.

Before You Begin

✔ **1** Create a PDF in Acrobat

See Also

→ **6** Insert Pages
→ **11** Add Headers and Footers

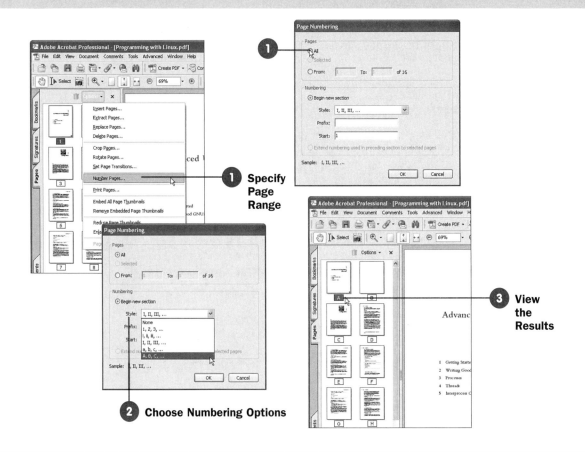

1 Specify Page Range

2 Choose Numbering Options

3 View the Results

3 View the Results

Click the **OK** button at the bottom of the **Page Numbering** dialog box to apply the new settings to your document. Use the **Previous Page** and **Next Page** buttons at the bottom of the document window to navigate through your document; you'll see that Acrobat displays the document with the new page numbers. (It lists the "real" page numbers in parentheses, as well.)

11 Add Headers and Footers

If your source document doesn't contain page numbers or other *header* or *footer* data, you can add your own to a PDF with the **Headers and Footers** command. Acrobat headers and footers not only allow you to add page numbers to your PDF, but also enable you to add a date field and other text, such as document name, file location, copyright information, or anything else you can think of.

Adding headers and footers in Acrobat is extremely useful if you are combining multiple documents together, especially if those documents come from different authoring applications.

1 Create Header and Footer Fields

From the **Document** menu, select the **Add Headers and Footers** command. This opens up the rather large **Add Headers and Footers** dialog box. At the top of the dialog box is a set of three boxes for different placements of header information (the three footer boxes can be accessed by clicking the **Footer** tab above the first box). Anything entered in the first box is left-aligned at the top of the page, anything entered in the second box is centered, and anything entered in the third box is right-aligned.

You can type header or footer data into these boxes, or you can insert date or page number fields. To enter a date or page number field, click in one of the boxes, select one of the date or page number formats from the **Insert Date** or **Insert Page Number** drop-down list, and click the appropriate **Insert** button. You can also format your header or footer data by selecting the text and then selecting a font and font size from the drop-down lists in the **Font** area of the dialog box.

2 Choose Page Options

At the top of the **Page Options** section of the **Add Headers and Footers** dialog box, specify to which pages you want the header and footer applied.

If you want the page numbering to start at a number other than 1, click the **Start Page Numbers at** check box and enter the number you want the page numbers to start at.

Before You Begin

✔ **1** Create a PDF in Acrobat

See Also

→ **2** Create a PDF from Multiple Files

→ **6** Insert Pages

→ **10** Renumber Pages

KEY TERMS

Header—Text or images that appear at the top of a range of printed pages.

Footer—Text or images that appear at the bottom of a range of printed pages.

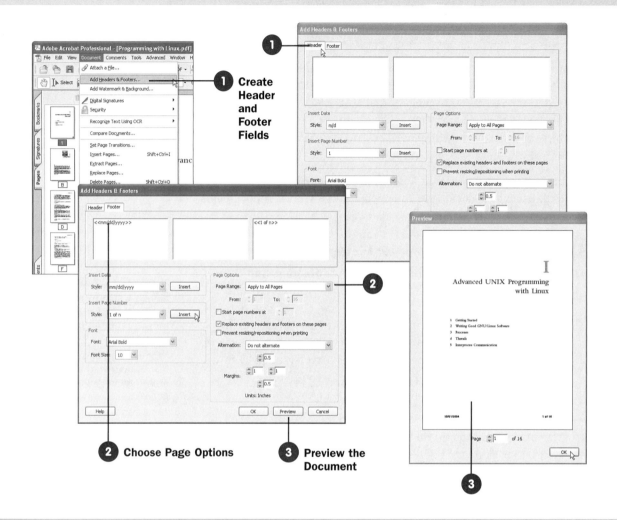

1 Create Header and Footer Fields

2 Choose Page Options

3 Preview the Document

If you want your header and footer to appear only on alternating pages (to create right-aligned page numbers for odd-numbered pages and left-aligned page numbers for even-numbered pages, for example), select **Even Pages Only** or **Odd Pages Only** from the **Alternation** drop-down list.

Finally, set the distance between your header and footer and the edge of the page in the top, bottom, left, and right **Margins** boxes.

3 Preview the Document

Click the **Preview** button at the bottom of the **Add Headers and Footers** dialog box. In the **Preview** dialog box that appears, click the up **Page** arrow or enter page numbers to see how the headers and footers will appear on various pages in your document. When you are done, click the **OK** button in this dialog box to exit the preview and then click the **OK** button in the **Add Headers and Footers** dialog box to apply your new headers and footers to your document.

12 Edit Text

If the PDF requires major changes to the text, you need to modify the original document in its original authoring application. You might want to do this anyway, so that future versions of the document will include any minor text changes you might be tempted to make in Acrobat. However, if all you need to do is make a quick edit or two to a PDF before sending it out, you can do so in Acrobat fairly quickly and easily. You can also change basic text formatting such as font, font size, and color.

One caveat to keep in mind is that you cannot do any editing or formatting of text in a PDF document unless you have the font used in the PDF installed on your computer or the author of the PDF has *embedded* the font in the PDF. See **Create a PDF in Acrobat** for details on how to embed fonts.

1 Select Text

From the **Tools** menu, select the **Advanced Editing, TouchUp Text Tool**. After selecting this tool, your cursor changes to a standard I-beam text selection cursor, which you are probably familiar with from MS Word or other text editing applications. Click a block of text to enter text edit mode for that block of text (a colored border appears around the text block); then click and drag across the desired text with the **TouchUp Text** tool cursor to select it.

Before You Begin

✔ **1** Create a PDF in Acrobat

Embedded fonts—Fonts whose information is stored within the PDF file itself. This ensures that the fonts displays and prints correctly even if the user does not have the fonts installed on her computer.

TIP

If you are going to be doing a lot of text editing, you'll be better off displaying the **Advanced Editing** toolbar (by selecting **View** menu, **Toolbars, Advanced Editing**) and clicking the **TouchUp Text** tool. Because you might be switching to other tools between edits, this makes reselecting the **TouchUp Text** tool easier each time you need to edit text.

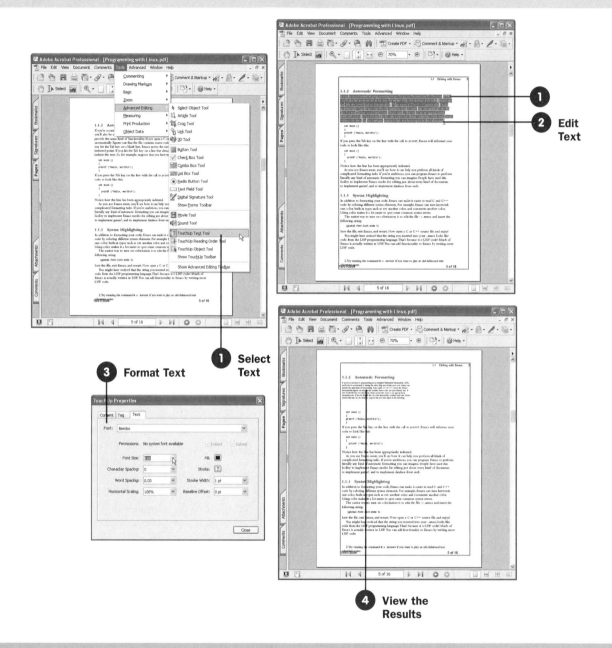

1 Select Text

2 Edit Text

3 Format Text

4 View the Results

② **Edit Text**

Edit the text normally, either by deleting the text and then typing new text or by highlighting a block of text and typing over it. Keep in mind that the **TouchUp Text** tool is for making small edits. Acrobat does not reflow multiline text changes.

③ **Format Text**

Selected text can be formatted by right-clicking (Windows) or Ctrl-clicking (Mac OS) the selected text and selecting the **Properties** command from the context menu. In the **TouchUp Properties** dialog box, click the **Text** tab. From here you can change the font, font size, and many other text attributes. When you are done, click the **Close** button to return to your document.

④ **View the Results**

View text changes in the document window. If you have made changes to text on multiple pages, press the **Page Down** key or click the **Next Page** button at the bottom of the document window. You can also zoom in or out of the document by selecting the **Zoom To** command located under the **View** menu. When the **Zoom To** dialog box appears, select a magnification and click the **OK** button.

 TIP

Another way to zoom in and out of a document view is to use the **Zoom** toolbar. If it's not already displayed, from the **View** menu, select **Toolbar**, **Zoom**. This opens the **Zoom** toolbar. Located on the **Zoom** toolbar are the **Zoom In Tool** drop-down menu; **Actual Size**, **Fit Page**, and **Fit Width** buttons; **Zoom Out** and **Zoom In** buttons; and a drop-down **Zoom In/Out** percentage box. Any of these tools or buttons can change the view of your PDF.

4

PDF Document Review

IN THIS CHAPTER:

Adobe Acrobat can play an integral part in the document review process. In fact, document review is one of the major selling points of Adobe Acrobat in the corporate market. Because the PDF file format maintains the formatting integrity of the source document, using Acrobat in the document review process has the added benefit that the reviewer can give design and layout feedback with a high assurance that he is seeing a true representation of what the source document looks like.

As the initiator of a PDF document review, you can send PDF documents for review and manage reviewers' comments with the review **Tracker**. You can also send email reminders to reviewers and invite others to review your document.

As a participant of a PDF document review, you can receive either an email-based or browser-based review, add your comments to a PDF document, view other reviewers' comments if the initiator has uploaded them for viewing, and even comment on the PDF document offline if you choose to work in Acrobat and not in a web browser. Acrobat's commenting tools allow you to place digital sticky notes on a PDF document to add your comments, highlight specific text that needs to be edited, indicate other edits with a pencil tool, and use the **Stamp** tool in the same way you would use a real rubber stamp on a document.

13 About the Review Process

KEY TERMS

Email-based reviews—A review process in which PDFs are sent by email to recipients for commenting as attachments.

Browser-based reviews—A review process in which the PDF is stored in one location, usually on a shared server, and accessed by the reviewers via a web browser.

Before sending off a PDF for review, you must first decide whether you want the review to be email-based or browser-based. *Email-based reviews* are ideal when you need to have clients, people outside your company, or anyone who does not have access to the same shared server review documents. *Browser-based reviews* require that all participants have access to the same shared server, but they have the advantage that comments are available to view by all reviewers during the review process. You might also choose to send the PDF document as a regular email attachment to each reviewer for commenting, but you need to manually keep track of the review and their comments. Acrobat does not automatically manage comments generated from this type of review.

Acrobat simplifies the document review process with setup wizards that walk you step-by-step through the process of setting up either an email-based or browser-based review. The **Tracker** helps you manage the review process by listing document reviews you've initiated along with a list of review participants, a list of reviews you are participating in, and any documents you have taken offline for review.

NOTE

Adobe Reader 7 now enables reviewers to participate in the document review process. It is recommended that the reviewer use Adobe Reader 7 when reviewing and commenting on a document originating from Acrobat 7.

Reviewers with older versions of Acrobat can participate in the document review process, but many features are unavailable to them if the original review process was initiated in Acrobat 7.

14 Email-Based Review

An email-based review of a PDF requires an email application, a mail server, and the PDF document to be reviewed. The reviewer receives the document as an attachment to an email, which she can download and view in Adobe Acrobat or Adobe Reader 7. When she is finished reviewing and commenting on the document, she clicks the **Send Comments** button to send it back to you.

This is not to be confused with manually attaching a PDF document to an email and sending it for review. An email-based review configures the PDF document for commenting and automatically displays any commenting tools the reviewer will need for the document. When she returns the reviewed document to you, Acrobat prompts you with a **Merge Comments?** dialog box. At that time, you can decide whether to have Acrobat merge comments into your document. Manually attaching a document to an email and then sending it to a reviewer does not make it a part of the reviewing process, so when the document is returned to you, you must manually migrate the reviewer's comments into your source review document.

Before You Begin

✔ **1** Create a PDF in Acrobat

✔ **4** Create PDFs from Microsoft Office

✔ **5** About Creating a PDF from Other Applications

See Also

→ **15** Browser-Based Review

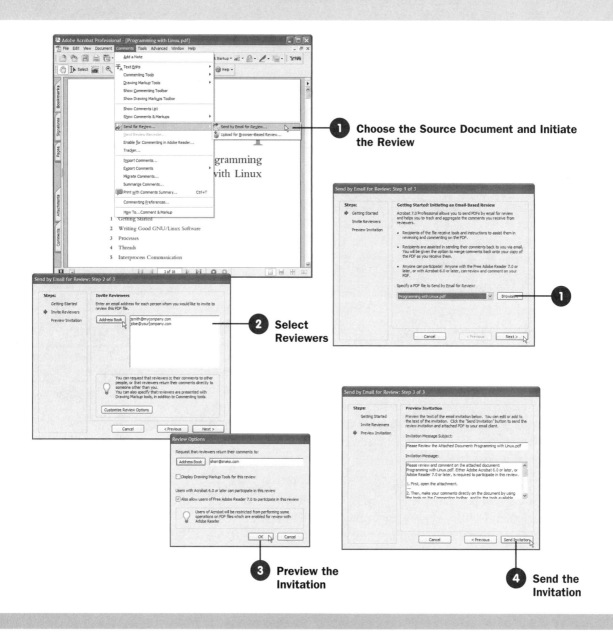

① Choose the Source Document and Initiate the Review

② Select Reviewers

③ Preview the Invitation

④ Send the Invitation

① Choose the Source Document and Initiate the Review

From the **File** menu, select **Open** and browse to the PDF document you want to send for review.

From the **Comments** menu, under the **Send for Review** submenu, select **Send by Email for Review**. This starts the **Send by Email for Review** setup wizard and present you with the **Step 1 of 3** dialog box for sending reviews by email. Acrobat always assumes the document that is open is the one you want to send for review and populates the **Specify a PDF File to Send by Email for Review** drop-down list with the name of the open file. If you want to send a different document, click the **Browse** button and then locate and open the file you want to send.

Click the **Next** button at the bottom of the dialog box to go to step 2.

② Select Reviewers

The **Send by Email for Review: Step 2 of 3** dialog box allows you to add email addresses for each reviewer. You either need to type or copy and paste the email addresses or need to type them manually into the space provided. If you need to look up someone's email address, click the **Address Book** button to launch your default email client so you can locate (and copy, if you want) the email address.

If you want to change the email review options, click the **Customize Review Options** button. This brings up the **Review Options** dialog box, where you can change the return email address to someone other than yourself or CC others. You can also select **Display Markup Tools for This Review** and **Allow Users of Free Adobe Reader 7 to Participate in This Review** if desired.

③ Preview the Invitation

The **Send by Email Review: Step 3 of 3** dialog box provides you with the subject line that includes the PDF filename and instructions for the reviewer on how to review and comment on the PDF. If you need to add your own comments to the instructions, just click in the text box and type in your comments.

④ Send the Invitation

When you click the **Send Invitation** button, Acrobat automatically attaches the PDF, populates your default email client with the subject line and instruction message, and then sends the email review to the reviewers. If your default email application does not automatically send the email, you need to manually send the message.

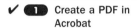

Browser-Based Review

Before You Begin

✔ **①** Create a PDF in Acrobat

✔ **④** Create PDFs from Microsoft Office

✔ **⑤** About Creating a PDF from Other Applications

See Also

→ **⑭** Email-Based Review

 NOTE

For a reviewer to partici-pate in a browser-based review that was initiated in Acrobat 7, he must use Adobe Acrobat 7. Older ver-sions of Acrobat allow for browser-based reviewing but do not support many of the features of Acrobat 7's browser-based reviews.

Adobe Reader 7 users can also participate in the browser-based review as long as additional user rights—such as filling in forms, participating in online reviews, and digitally signing documents—have been included in the PDF document. If additional user rights have been included in the PDF docu-ment for review, a yellow Document Messenger Bar appears displaying the additional reviewing tools.

A browser-based review requires that the PDF document reside on a serv-er that is accessible to both you and your reviewers. After the reviewer receives the review invitation email and opens the attachment, a copy of the PDF document opens in a web browser. After reviewing the docu-ment and adding comments, the reviewer then uploads them to an online comments repository designated by the initiator in the docu-ment's preferences. Reviewers can view comments made by other review-ers and reply to them, but they cannot edit or delete another's comments.

① Choose the Source Document

From the **Comments** menu, under the **Send for Review** submenu, select the **Upload for Browser-Based Review** command. In the **Initiate an On-line Review: Step 1 of 4** dialog box, click the **Browse** button to locate the PDF file to be reviewed. Select the PDF file, and then click **Next** to go to the next step.

② Upload the Document to the Server

Click the **Browse** button to specify where you want to save the PDF file on the server. Be sure to save the file on a server that is accessi-ble by all reviewers.

If Acrobat has not automatically configured the location of your review comment repository, click the **Configure** button. This opens the **On-Line Commenting Auto Configuration** dialog box. Enter the comment repository that is provided by your system adminis-trator.

Click **Next** to go to step 3.

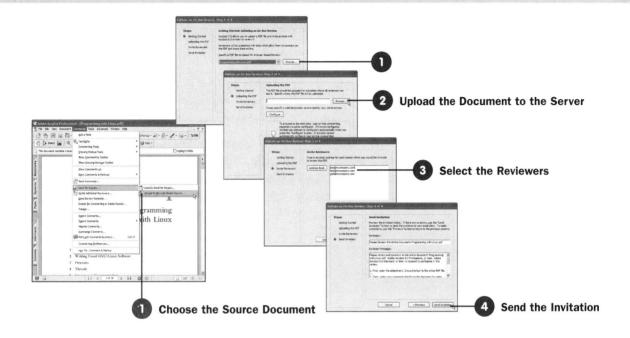

Upload the Document to the Server

Select the Reviewers

Choose the Source Document

Send the Invitation

3 **Select the Reviewers**

The **Initiate an On-Line Review: Step 3 of 4** dialog box allows you to add email addresses for each reviewer. You need to either type or copy and paste the email addresses into the space provided, or type them in manually. If you need to look up someone's email address, click the **Address Book** button to launch your default email client so you can locate (and copy, if you want) the email address.

Click **Next** to go to the final step.

NOTE

Before sending a browser-based review, you need to make sure you have the correct server settings. Under the **Edit** menu, select **Preferences** to bring up the **Preferences** dialog box. Under the topic heading **Categories**, click **Reviewing**. Select the type of server to which you will be uploading the PDF document, along with any other server settings needed for the review, such as **Confirm Importing of Annots into Active Reviews from PDF Files, Open the Comment List When Comments Are Imported**, and **Automatically Open Toolbars for Reviews.** If you are unsure of the proper server settings, contact your system administrator.

TIP

If you add comments to your PDF document before uploading it to the server for browser-based reviewing, your comments will be embedded in the document and you will no longer be able to edit them.

 TIP

When using a browser to review a document, unsaved comments are lost when you visit another website. Be sure to always click the **Send and Receive** button in the **Commenting** toolbar to save your comments.

 TIP

You can add comments to a PDF document while working offline. Just click the **Save and Work Offline** button on the **Comments** toolbar in the browser window to download the PDF document to a specified location. After you have finished reviewing the document in Acrobat, click the **Go Back Online** button on the **Comments** toolbar. This closes Acrobat and reopens the browser window.

④ Send the Invitation

The **Initiate an On-Line Review: Step 4 of 4** dialog box provides the subject line that includes the location of the PDF filename and instructions for the reviewer on how to review and comment on the PDF. If you need to add your own comments to the instructions, just click in the text box and type in your comments.

When you click the **Send Invitation** button at the bottom of the dialog box, Acrobat automatically populates your default email client with the subject line and instruction message and then sends the email review to the reviewers. If your default email application does not automatically send the email, you need to manually send the message.

16 About Review Tracker

Before You Begin

✔ **14** Email-Based Review

✔ **15** Browser-Based Review

The **Tracker** manages all PDF documents that have been sent and received for both email- and browser-based reviews, including any documents you have reviewed offline. The **Tracker** automatically places the documents in one of three folders: **My Reviews** contains PDF documents you have sent for review, **Participant Reviews** contains PDF documents that have been sent to you for review, and **Offline Documents** contains PDF documents you have taken offline for review. At any time, you can create a new folder and move the documents.

PART I: Covering the Basics

The Tracker window.

If you have initiated a document review, the **Tracker** can check the status on a review, send email reminders to reviewers, and invite additional reviewers. The **Tracker** also lists all the PDFs you have initiated for review, including the type of review it was. To find out more information on a particular PDF review, click the PDF link; the **Tracker** displays the PDF filename, the type of review, the date and time the review was sent, and the list of emails of who the review was sent to.

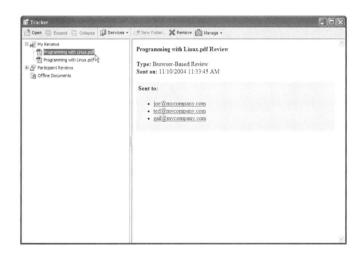

A list of current PDFs to be reviewed, which you have initiated.

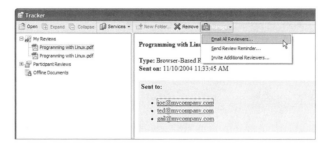

Send an email reminder to reviewers.

If you are a participant in a review, the **Tracker** lists all the PDF documents you are reviewing. When you select a PDF document you are currently reviewing, the **Tracker** displays the type of review it is, the date
and time at which it was sent, who initiated the review, the location of
your PDF document, and all the other participating reviewers.

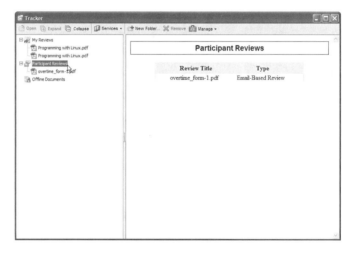

A list of PDFs you are currently reviewing.

17 Add Note Comments

The simplest and most common way to annotate a PDF document is to add note comments. These appear as tiny Post-It-style notes in the PDF. Mousing over the note displays the note's content, which is the actual comment itself. Notes can be deleted by clicking them with the **Hand** tool and pressing the **Delete** or **Backspace** key.

1 Select the Note Tool

Before adding any comment to a PDF, you must first select the appropriate commenting tool. In this case, that's the **Note** tool. You can select the **Note** tool directly by clicking the **Tools** menu and selecting **Commenting**, **Note Tool**. If you are going to be doing a lot of annotating, you should display the **Commenting** toolbar, which gives you easy access to several commenting tools. You can display this toolbar by clicking the **Tools** menu and selecting **Commenting**, **Show Commenting Toolbar** (located at the bottom of the menu).

2 Place the Note

Click or near the item you want to comment on. A note icon appears in the document at that location and a small window opens on the right side of the document that points back to the icon. Both the icon and the window can be easily repositioned by simply clicking the icon or the title bar of the window with the **Hand** tool and dragging either one to a new position.

3 Add Comments

Type your comments into the note window. If you need to reopen a note's comment window, simply double-click the note icon. You can also select text and use the **Options** menu in the upper-right corner of the comment window to do basic text editing and formatting. Click the close box of the comment window to close it when you are done entering your comments.

See Also

→ **21** Import Comments to a PDF

→ **22** Export Comments from a PDF

→ **23** Export Comments to Word

→ **25** Summarize Comments in a PDF

 TIP

To give you an idea of how many note-type comments are added to a document compared to all other comment types, the first command in the **Comments** menu is **Add a Note**. It is the only comment type that appears in the main **Comments** menu, and it is the only comment type that can be added directly from a menu (all other comments must be added by selecting the appropriate tool and then clicking in the document). Selecting this command places a note in the middle of the document window. You can move this note as desired by dragging it to a new location.

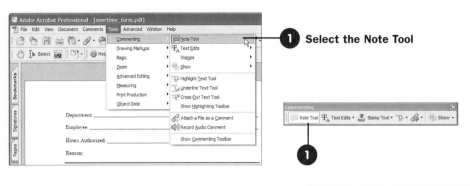

1 Select the Note Tool

2 Place the Note

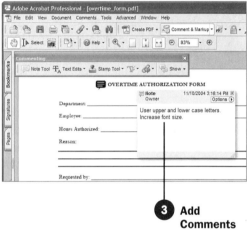

3 Add
Comments

18 Apply Document Status and Other Graphical Stamps

Before You Begin

✔ **17** Add Note
Comments

See Also

→ **25** Summarize
Comments in
a PDF

Acrobat provides numerous graphical stamps that you can add to a document in much the same way you would rubberstamp a physical document. These stamps include everything from **Void** and **Confidential** to **Sign Here**, and they can include dynamic approval date and time information. Using these stamps makes it easier than ever to incorporate Acrobat into your business processes or document review workflow.

1 Open a Review Document

3 Apply a Stamp

2 Select a Stamp

3

4 Add Comments

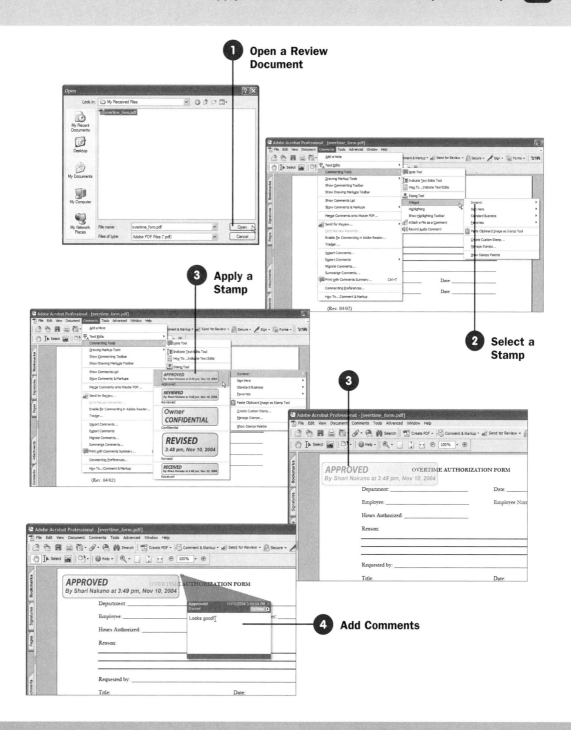

NOTE

You can create your own personal stamp in Acrobat. From the **Tools** menu, select **Commenting, Stamps, Create Custom Stamps**.

This opens the **Select Image for Custom Stamp** dialog box. Click the **Browse** button to locate and open the file you want to use for the stamp. You can create a stamp image from a large variety of supported file formats, such as PDF, JPEG, bitmap, Adobe Illustrator (AI), Adobe Photoshop (PSD), and Autodesk AutoCAD (DWT, DWG). After you have selected the image or document, Acrobat displays it in the **Sample** window box. Click the **OK** button to go to the **Create Custom Stamp** dialog box. You can then enter the name of your new stamp and select an existing category or create a new category for your new stamp.

TIP

If you find yourself using the **Stamp** tools on a regular basis, you can open the **Stamps Palette** window for quick and easy access to the stamps. From the **Comments** menu, select **Commenting Tools, Stamp Tool, Show Stamp Palette**. After the **Stamps** palette window is open, click and drag the appropriate stamp onto your document.

① Open a Review Document

Under the **File** menu, select the **Open** command to locate and open the PDF document to be reviewed.

② Select a Stamp

From the **Comments** menu, select **Commenting Tools, Stamps**. Then, from the **Dynamic**, **Sign Here**, and **Standard Business** categories submenu, select the stamp you want to place in the PDF document.

The **Standard Business** category contains standard business stamps, such as **Draft**, **Final**, and **Confidential**. The **Sign Here** category contains typical contract callouts such as **Sign Here**, **Accepted**, and **Rejected**. The **Dynamic** category uses several of the stamps from the **Standard Business** category but inserts the username and current date and time.

③ Apply a Stamp

Selecting a stamp from the menu changes your cursor to a translucent version of the stamp. With this cursor, click in your document where you want the stamp to be placed.

④ Add Comments

If you want to add comments to the stamp, double-click the stamp to open the stamp's pop-up comment window. Type your comments into the window and click the window's close box when you are done.

19 Add Text Editing Comments

Text edits are handled differently from other types of comments. Instead of selecting a commenting tool, clicking in your document to place some sort of marker, and then entering your comments in a separate window, you basically make text edits as you would in a word processor and Acrobat marks the text appropriately. For example, if you select a block of text and press the **Backspace** or **Delete** key, the text is marked for deletion as indicated by a red line through the selected text. On the other hand, if you click somewhere in your text and start typing, a text insertion marker is added to indicate where the new text should be inserted. Regardless of the type of text edit, if you hold the mouse over the text edit indicator, a pop-up appears, displaying the additional or changed text or any comments associated with that text.

See Also

→ **17** Add Note Comments

→ **20** Add Drawing Markups to a PDF

→ **25** Summarize Comments in a PDF

1 Open the Review Document and Select the Text Edit Tool

Under the **File** menu, select the **Open** command to locate and open the PDF document to be reviewed. If the PDF document is part of a review process sent to you for review, Acrobat automatically opens the **Commenting** toolbar.

Under the **Comments** menu, select **Text Edits, Indicate Text Edits Tool**. Acrobat displays a dialog box explaining the basics of indicating text insertion, deletion, and replacement comments. Read the instructions and click the **OK** button. If you do not want to see this dialog box each time you do text edits, click the **Don't Show Again** check box.

2 Indicate Standard Text Edits

Using the text edit cursor, make changes to your text just as you would in a word processing application. To indicate a text deletion, select a block of text and press **Backspace** or **Delete**. To indicate replacement text, select a block of text and type the new text. To indicate new text to be inserted, click to place an insertion point and type the new text to be added.

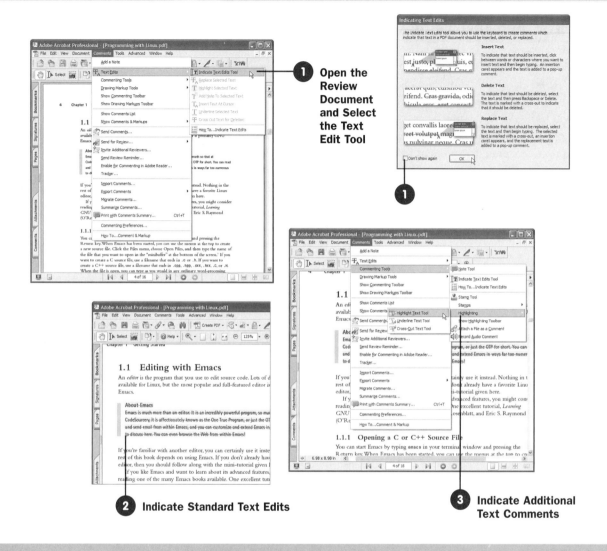

1 Open the Review Document and Select the Text Edit Tool

2 Indicate Standard Text Edits

3 Indicate Additional Text Comments

3 Indicate Additional Text Comments

The **Text Edits** submenu also contains commands for calling attention to specific blocks of text. You can highlight, underline, or add a note to selected text. To do so, simply select the desired block of text and then select **Highlight Selected Text**, **Add Note to Selected Text**, or **Underline Selected Text** from the **Text Edits** submenu.

20 Add Drawing Markups to a PDF

Whereas the standard commenting tools are typically used for text-heavy documents, the drawing markup tools are well-suited for design-heavy documents, such as flow charts, engineering specs, presentations, ad proposals, and other documents that contain visual information. This does not mean the drawing markup tools cannot be used on text documents. Acrobat's drawing markup tools are ideal any time it is easier to show a change rather than explain it. Many of the drawing tools enable you to point to a specific location in a document instead of having to try to describe where a change needs to be made.

See Also

→ **17** Add Note Comments

→ **19** Add Text Editing Comments

→ **25** Summarize Comments in a PDF

① Open the Review Document and Select a Markup Tool

Under the **File** menu, select the **Open** command to locate and open the PDF document to be reviewed.

From the **Tools** menu, click the **Drawing Markups** submenu and select one of the drawing markup tools. The drawing markup submenu is divided into two sections. The top section contains the **Callout**, **Cloud**, **Dimension**, and **Text Box** tools. The bottom section contains the **Arrow**, **Rectangle**, **Oval**, **Line**, **Polygon Line**, **Polygon**, **Pencil**, and **Pencil Eraser** tools. The tools in the top section create markups that consist of both graphical and text components, whereas the tools in the bottom section are primarily graphical in nature. Selecting any of these tools changes your cursor to a crosshair, which you will be using in the next step.

② Add Comments

With the crosshair drawing markup cursor, click and drag to define the dimensions or direction of the drawing markup graphic. If you selected one of the tools from the top section, type in your comments as well. If you selected one of the tools from the bottom section, additional comments are not expected. However, you can add comments to any of the graphics created by the tools in the bottom section by double-clicking the graphic itself and typing your comments into the pop-up comment window.

Open the Review Document and Select a Markup Tool

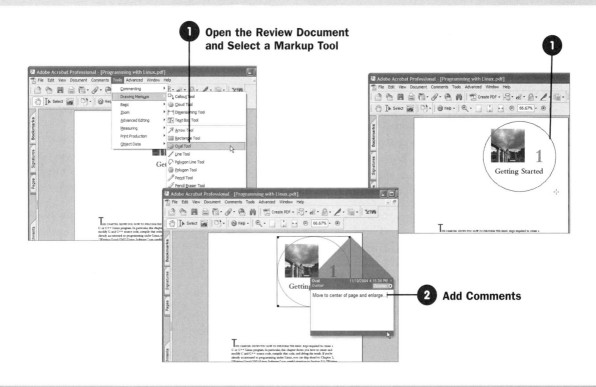

Add Comments

21 Import Comments to a PDF

Before You Begin

✔ **17** Add Note Comments

✔ **19** Add Text Editing Comments

See Also

→ **22** Export Comments from a PDF

→ **23** Export Comments to Word

→ **25** Summarize Comments in a PDF

After reviewers have added their comments to your PDF document and returned it to you, you need to combine all the reviewer comments into your original PDF document.

1 Open the Review Document and Merge Comments

From the **File** menu, select the **Open** command to locate and open the PDF document that was used for the review.

From the **File** menu, select **Comments**, **Migrate Comments**. The **Migrate Comments** dialog box appears and prompts you to enter the reviewer's returned document. Click the **Choose** button to locate the document and click the **OK** button. This merges the reviewer's comments to your original review document. To add other reviewers' comments to your document, repeat this step until all the comments have been added to your document.

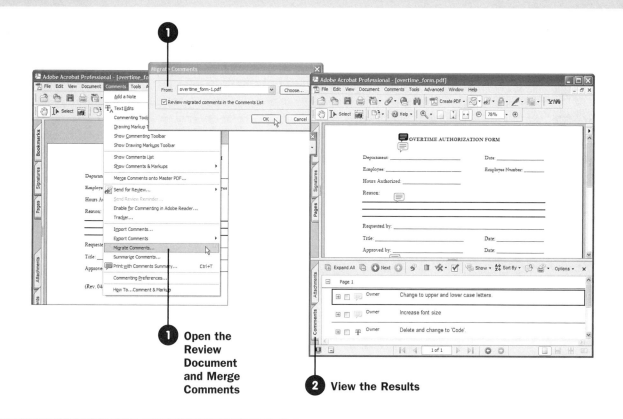

1 Open the
Review
Document
and Merge
Comments

2 View the Results

2 View the Results

To view the comments, click the **Comments** tab located on the left
side of the document window. This opens the **Comments** pane and
displays all the comments in your document. Comments are indicated on your document by a number of different comment icons,
such as Post-It-type icons, highlighted or marked text, a stamp
icon, or even a sound clip icon.

You can sort comments by author, color, check mark status, date,
page, status by person, or type of comment. The color of a comment indicates the type of comment it is, whether it is a note,
highlighted, deleted (Cross-out), a stamp, or an underlined type
comment. The check mark status can be used to keep track of comments already read or responded to, or it can indicate anything
you want it to.

22 Export Comments from a PDF

Before You Begin

✔ **17** Add Note Comments

✔ **19** Add Text Editing Comments

See Also

→ **21** Import Comments to a PDF

→ **23** Export Comments to Word

→ **25** Summarize Comments in a PDF

When exporting comments from a PDF document, Acrobat creates a new Form Data Format (FDF) file that contains just those comments. You can then send the FDF file to other reviewers who then import it into a PDF document to view. FDF files are smaller than normal PDF documents and cannot be opened on their own. They must be imported into an existing PDF document to be viewed.

1 Open a Review Document and Export Comments

From the **File** menu, select the **Open** command, locate the PDF document with existing comments and open the document.

From the **Comments** menu, select **Export Comments**, **To File**. This opens the **Export Comments** dialog box. Navigate to the location where you want to save the comments file and enter a new filename. Under the **Save As type** drop-down menu (Windows) or **Select** menu (Mac OS), select the **Acrobat FDF Files (*.fdf)** type; then click **Save**.

2 Send a File

After the comments have been exported to the FDF file, you can send them to other reviewers to import into their PDF documents. Simply attach the FDF file to an email or upload it to a shared server for the reviewer to access. The reviewer can then download and import the file into the PDF document.

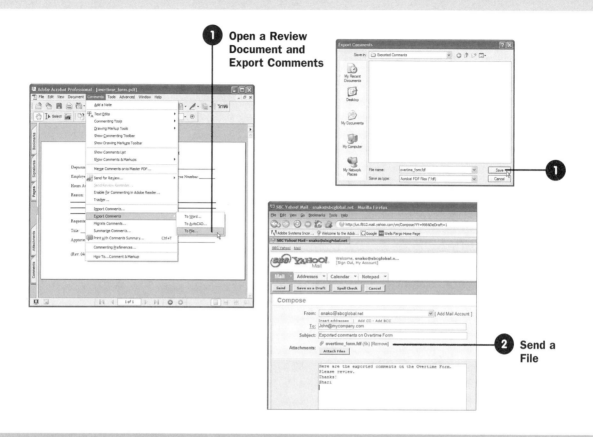

1 Open a Review Document and Export Comments

2 Send a File

23 Export Comments to Word

If your original source document was created in Word, Acrobat can export comments from the PDF file and integrate those comments and text edits into your original Word document. (This feature is available only for Windows users.) The advantage of exporting comments to Word is that you do not have to switch back and forth between the comments in the PDF document and making the changes in the Word document.

Before You Begin

✔ **17** Add Note Comments

✔ **19** Add Text Editing Comments

See Also

→ **21** Import Comments to a PDF

→ **22** Export Comments from a PDF

→ **25** Summarize Comments in a PDF

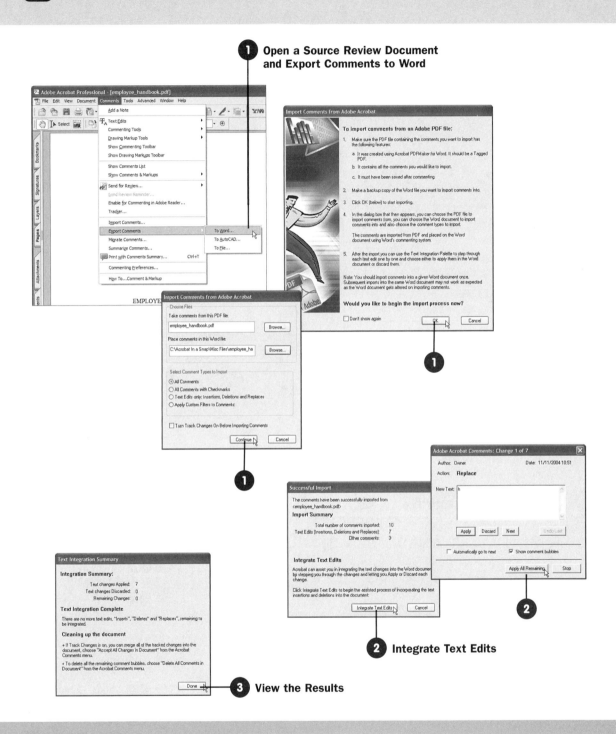

1 Open a Source Review Document and Export Comments to Word

2 Integrate Text Edits

3 View the Results

PART I: Web Authoring

1 Open a Source Review Document and Export Comments to Word

From the **File** menu, select the **Open** command, locate a Word-based PDF document with existing comments, and open the document. If this document is part of a review process, make sure that all comments are merged into one PDF before exporting them to Word.

From the **Comments** menu, select **Export Comments, To Word**. Acrobat launches Microsoft Word and displays the **Import Comments from Adobe Acrobat** dialog box. Read through the **How the Import Process Works** instructions; then click the **OK** button to proceed.

A different **Import Comments from Adobe Acrobat** dialog box appears, confirming from which PDF document the comments are being taken and which Word file they are being placed in. Acrobat automatically populates these fields with the open PDF document and corresponding Word document. If you need to change either the PDF or Word document, click the **Browse** button, locate the correct file, and open it. The dialog box also prompts you to select the type of comments to import: **All Comments, All Comments with Checkmarks, Text Edits Only: Insertions and Deletions**, and **Apply Custom Filters to Comments**. At the bottom of the dialog box, you can choose to enable track changes in the Word document before importing the comments. Click the **Continue** button to export comments.

2 Integrate Text Edits

If your comments include any text edits, Acrobat allows you to integrate any text changes into your Word document. In the **Successful Import** dialog box, click the **Integrate Text Edits** button. This opens the Adobe Acrobat Comments: Change X of X dialog box, where you can choose to either apply or discard the edits. You can also apply all edit changes by clicking the **Apply All Remaining** button at the bottom of the dialog box. A confirmation box appears, asking whether you want to apply all text changes and skip the rest of the integration process. Click **OK** to continue.

NOTE

If you try to export comments from a PDF document into a Word document that has been modified or edited since the creation of the PDF, comments and text edits from the PDF might be misplaced or otherwise improperly imported into the Word document. For this reason, be sure to always work with a PDF of the most recent version of the Word document.

3 View the Results

A **Text Integration Summary** dialog box appears after the comments have been added and any text edits made. The summary includes how many text changes were applied, how many text changes were discarded, and whether any changes remain. Your Word document now has comments and text edits integrated into it, just as if the commenting and editing were originally done in that document.

24 About the Comments Pane

Before You Begin

✓ **17** Add Note Comments

✓ **18** Apply Document Status and Other Graphical Stamps

✓ **19** Add Text Editing Comments

✓ **20** Add Drawing Markups to a PDF

See Also

→ **25** Summarize Comments in a PDF

The **Comments** pane organizes and keeps track of all comments made in a PDF document during the review process. Unlike other navigation panes in Acrobat, which are displayed along the left side of the document window, when you click the **Comments** tab, the **Comments** pane is displayed at the bottom of the document window. This horizontal orientation makes a lot more sense for displaying potentially long comments.

The Comments pane.

Starting on the left side of the **Comments** pane are the **Expand All** and **Collapse All** elements buttons. Next to that are up and down arrow buttons which, when clicked, move the focus to the previous or next comment.

The **Reply** button attaches a response to a reviewer's comments. Select the comment you want to reply to and click the **Reply** button. Acrobat populates your reply comment with your name, the comment it is regarding, and the date and time. You can then add a response by clicking to the right of the comment header information (name, title, and so on) and typing your reply.

The trash can icon deletes selected comments from the list. Select the comment you want to delete and click the trash can.

Set Status sets the comment's review or migration status. For review comments, they can be marked as **Accepted**, **Rejected**, **Cancelled**, or **Completed**. For migration comments, they can be marked **Not-Confirmed** or **Confirmed**.

The check mark can be used to indicate almost anything you want it to. For example, you can mark any comments you have yet to read or even keep track of comments you have already read.

Under the **Show** menu on the **Comments** menu, you can choose to hide or show comments and show comments by type, reviewer, status, or checked state. You can also choose to show the **Comments** and **Drawing Markup** toolbars.

Display comments by a specific type.

Comments can be sorted by type, page, author, date, color, check mark status, or status by person in the **Comments** pane. Simply click the **Sort By** command to make your sorting selection and Acrobat reorganizes the comments in the order you've chosen.

You can also search all the comments for a particular word or phrase. Click the **Search** comments button to open the **Search PDF** panel. Enter a word or phrase to search for, and click the radio button next to **Whole Word Only** or **Case Sensitive** if you need look for specific words or cases. Click the **Search Comments** button to have Acrobat search through all the comments for the word or phrase and display them in the **Results** window. Click the result to locate the comment in the document.

The Search Comments window.

The **Comments** pane also enables you to print the comments from you PDF document. Select the **Print Comments** command to do one of the following: **Print Comments Summary**, **Create PDF of Comments Summary**, or **More Options** to bring up the **Summarize Options** dialog box.

Other functions the **Comments** pane can perform are importing and exporting comments, summarizing comments, and launching the **Track Reviews** window. Click the **Options** button to display the various comment options.

25 Summarize Comments in a PDF

After the reviewers have added their comments to your PDF document, you can collect all their comments into a new, easy-to-read PDF you can print out and use as a reference while editing your original source document.

Before You Begin

✔ **17** Add Note Comments

✔ **19** Add Text Editing Comments

See Also

→ **14** Email-Based Review

→ **15** Browser-Based Review

→ **16** About Review Tracker

1 Select a Comment Summary Option

From the **Comments** menu, select the **Print Document with Comments Summary** command. This opens the **Summarize Options** dialog box.

2 Select a Layout

In the **Summarize Options** dialog box, you can choose from four layouts to print the PDF document and comments: **Document and Comments with Connector Lines on Separate Pages**, **Document and Comments with Connector Lines on Single Pages**, **Comments Only**, or **Document and Comments with Sequence Numbers on Separate Pages**. Click the radio button next to the layout to make your selection. A preview example of each layout appears.

Other options to choose from are the paper size; sorting comments by author, date, page, or type; whether to include all comments in the document or just the comments currently showing on the page; and the font size of the printed text.

3 View the Comment Summary

After you have made your selection as to how you want to display the document and comments, click the **OK** button to print the comments summary.

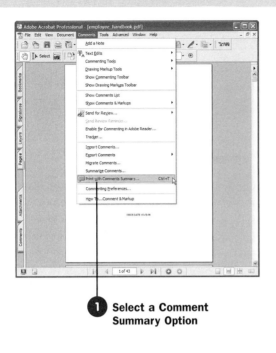

1 Select a Comment Summary Option

2 Select a Layout

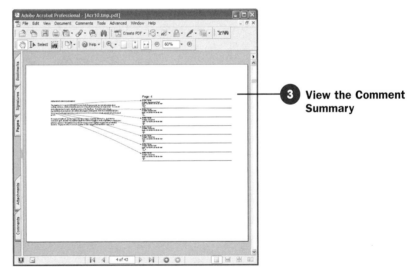

3 View the Comment Summary

PART II

Beyond
the Basics

IN THIS PART:

5

Document Security and Digital Signatures

IN THIS CHAPTER:

KEY TERM

Digital signature—A
unique digital identifier that
enables a user to certify
that a document has been
created, reviewed, or
approved. Digital signatures
are used in much the same
way that handwritten signatures are used.

NOTE

VeriSign and Entrust are
the two main providers
Adobe recommends for
using when creating a digital signature. Learn more
by going to VeriSign
(www.verisign.com) or
Entrust (www.entrust.com).

With the increasing amount of Acrobat users, document security has
become ever more important. When creating a PDF file, you can choose
to set restrictions on whether the file can be opened, edited, or printed.
Protection of your PDF files is done using a password, a certificate, or
Adobe Policy Server.

In addition to adding security to a PDF document, secure *digital signatures* can be included. By using a certified signature, you can rest
assured that your original PDF is not changed without your consent. You
can create a digital ID for signing with Acrobat or use a third-party signature provider such as VeriSign.

26 Secure a PDF File with Password Protection

See Also

→ **28** Create a Digital ID

→ **30** Add a Digital ID
Signature

By default, new PDF files are not secure. This means that anyone can
open, view, print, or make changes to the file. Adding password protection allows you to limit who can open the file, as well as what they can
do with it once they have it open. Acrobat provides both powerful and
flexible document security, giving you a wide variety of options, including opening the file; printing, copying, and extracting data; adding
comments; filling in form data; altering forms; providing access for the
disabled; and setting a level of encryption.

① **View Security Settings**

From the **File** menu, select **Document Properties**. In the
Document Properties dialog box, click the **Security** tab. This tab
is divided into two sections. The **Document Security** section contains controls for changing the document's security settings, whereas the **Document Restrictions Summary** section lets you know
what the viewer will and will not be allowed to do with the current
security settings.

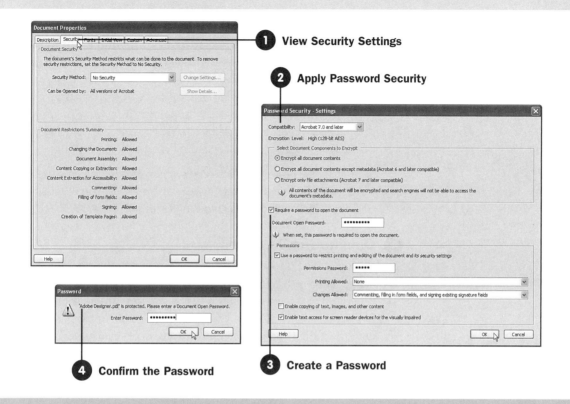

4 Confirm the Password

3 Create a Password

2 Apply Password Security

From the **Security Method** pop-up, select **Password Security**. This launches the **Password Security - Settings** dialog box. In the **Compatibility** drop-down list, select **Acrobat 7 and Later**. This ensures the highest encryption level. In the **Select Document Components to Encrypt** section, select whether you want to encrypt all document contents (the default option), all document contents except metadata, or only file attachments.

3 Create a Password

If you want to prevent anyone from opening the document without a password, click the **Require a Password to Open the Document** check box and enter a password in the **Document Open Password** field.

If you want to restrict what someone can do with the document, click the **Use a Password to Restrict Printing and Editing of the Document and Its Security Settings** check box and enter a password in the **Permissions Password** field. Select which types of printing and changes you want to allow from the **Printing Allowed** and **Changes Allowed** drop-down lists. Click the appropriate check boxes to enable or disable copying the contents of the document or text access for screen readers.

Note that you can apply both open password and permission password protection to the same document. You must use different passwords for each of these types of document protection.

④ Confirm the Password

Click the **OK** button to apply your password protection. You are immediately prompted to confirm your password. If you set a document open password, enter it in the **Document Open Password** field and click the **OK** button. If you set a permissions password, enter it in the **Permissions Password** field and click the **OK** button. Click **OK** at the third party and save reminder dialog boxes that appear.

To test the passwords, save the file and then close and reopen it. Enter the correct password to open the file. To change security settings, click the **File** menu and select **Document Properties**. In the **Document Properties** dialog box, click the **Security** tab and click the **Change Settings** button. You are prompted for the document's permissions password. Enter it and you are able to remove or modify the document's security settings.

 TIP

When choosing a password, try to make it unique. Incorporate letters and numbers so only you will know the password. Make sure the password is one you will remember, or write it down and keep it in a secret place. Too many people use family, friends, or pet names that make their password easy to guess.

---

27 Change Security Permissions

Before You Begin

✔ **26** Secure a PDF File with Password Protection

See Also

→ **60** Create an Accessible PDF

After you set the security for a PDF, you can always go back in and adjust the permissions options. If other people are accessing the file, you might want to protect just how much they can do to the PDF file. After you check the **Use a Password to Restrict Printing and Editing of the Document and Its Security Settings**, you have to enter a different password for the permissions. The first password you entered was just to open the file.

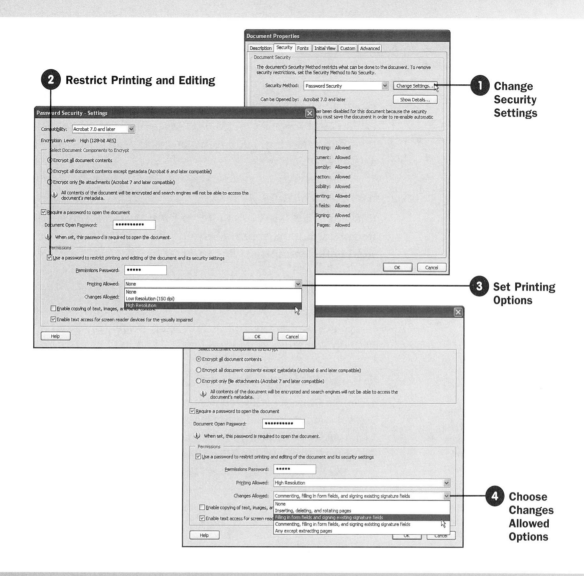

2 **Restrict Printing and Editing**

1 Change
Security
Settings

3 Set Printing
Options

4 Choose
Changes
Allowed
Options

Under the **Permissions** options, you can set the **Printing Allowed**
(**None**, **Low**, or **High Resolution**). Here you can set whether any printing is allowed and the resolution of the printing you permit.

In the **Changes Allowed** options, you set how much can be edited,
deleted, copied, or commented on in the document. Other check box
options are **Enable Copying of Text, Images, or Other Content** and

Enable Text Access for Screen Reader Devices for the Visually Impaired.

❶ Change Security Settings

Under the **File** menu, select **Document Properties**. In the **Document Properties** dialog box, select the **Security** tab and click the **Change Settings** button. This opens the **Password Security - Settings** dialog box.

❷ Restrict Printing and Editing

Click the **Use a Password to Restrict Printing and Editing of the document and Its Security Settings** check box and enter a password in the **Permissions Password** field.

❸ Set Printing Options

Under the **Printing Allowed** pop-up menu, select the type of printing you want to allow for this PDF. Select **None**, **Low Resolution (150 dpi)**, or **High Resolution**.

☝ TIP

When setting up permissions on your file, select your options wisely. For example, if you're sending a file that contains high-quality photographs, allow printing only at low resolution. This prevents the viewer from printing and possibly repurposing your photographs without your permission.

❹ Choose Changes Allowed Options

From the **Changes Allowed** pop-up menu, select how much editing you want to allow for this file. Select **None**; **Inserting, Deleting, and Rotating Pages**; **Filling In Form Fields and Signing**; **Commenting, Filling In Form Fields, and Signing**; or **Any Except Extracting Pages**. The final two check boxes let you select whether to permit copying areas of the PDF and to enable text access for the screen reader for visually impaired users.

28 Create a Digital ID

See Also

→ **29** Delete a Digital ID

→ **30** Add a Digital ID Signature

Electronic signatures have become even more popular and secure since e-Sign legislation was passed in 2000. Digital signatures are a great solution for paperless document reviewing. A digital signature not only validates the PDF, but also validates with Acrobat the identity of the person signing it. You can also digitally certify a document, which lets you know whether a document has been altered or tampered with.

1 Create a Digital ID

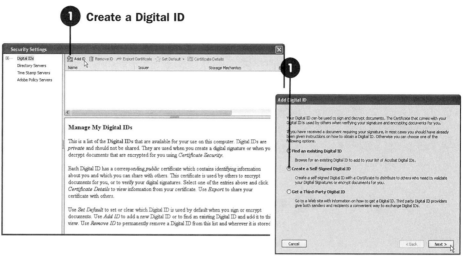

2 Select an ID Storage Option

3 Input Identifying Information

4 Enter Your Password

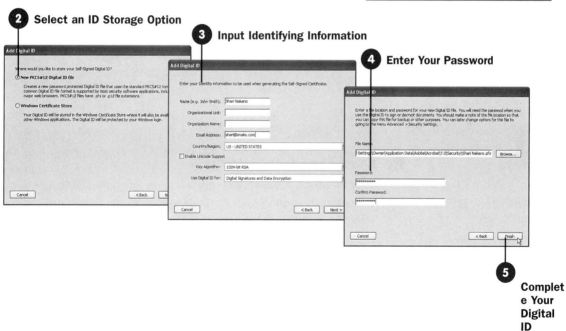

5 Complete Your Digital ID

Use Acrobat's digital ID to create and verify your signature.

① Create a Digital ID

Select **Advanced, Security Settings**. This launches the **Security Settings** dialog box. From this dialog box, click the **Add ID** button to add a digital ID. The **Add Digital ID** assistant appears, helping you through the steps to add a digital ID. Select **Create a Self-Signed Digital ID**. By creating a self-signed digital ID, you are the only one certified to use this ID. Click the **Next** button to bring up an information screen that informs you that you are about to create a digital ID. Click the **Next** button to go to the next screen.

② Select an ID Storage Option

Specify how you want to store your digital ID file by selecting one of the following options:

- **New PKCS#12 Digital ID File**—Stores your digital ID in the standard PKCS#12 encryption format.

- **Windows Certificate Store**—Stores your digital ID in the Windows Certificate Store, so it is then available for use with other Windows applications.

Click the **Next** button to proceed to the next screen.

③ Input Identifying Information

Type your name, organizational unit, organization name, email address, and country/region into the appropriate fields. You can select **Enable Unicode Support** if applicable. Select a key algorithm. The **1024-bit RSA** option is more compatible but less secure than **2048-bit RSA**.

Select one of the following for the **Use Digital ID for** option: **Digital Signatures**, **Data Encryption**, and **Digital Signatures and Data Encryption**. Click the **Next** button to proceed to the next screen.

④ Enter Your Password

Accept the default filename and location, or browse to the location where you want to save your digital ID. Enter a password for your new digital ID in both the **Password** and **Confirm Password** text boxes.

5 Complete Your Digital ID

In the assistant, click the **Finish** button to complete the creation of your new digital ID. The information then appears in the **Security Settings** dialog box.

 TIP

Other options with digital IDs are to save the data information or email the information to someone else. Exporting your digital ID as a file and then emailing it to someone allows the recipient to encrypt documents for you and validate signatures you have created. To do this, select the digital ID and click the **Export Certificate** button in the **Security Settings** dialog box

29 Delete a Digital ID

Removing digital IDs is required when you have changed your identifying information or when employees have changed jobs or companies. When managing your IDs, it is critical that you have the most up-to-date information.

Before You Begin

✔ **28** Create a Digital ID

1 Remove a Digital ID

Select **Advanced**, **Security Settings**. This launches the **Security Settings** dialog box.

Select the digital ID you want to remove by clicking it in the **Digital ID** list. Click the **Remove ID** button. A warning dialog box appears asking whether you are sure you want to remove the selected ID from your digital IDs file. This gives you a chance to make sure you chose the right digital ID to remove.

TIP

If you are unsure about deleting a digital ID, export the data so you have it saved. You can always add it back later.

2 Confirm the Deletion

Click the **OK** button to remove the digital ID you selected.

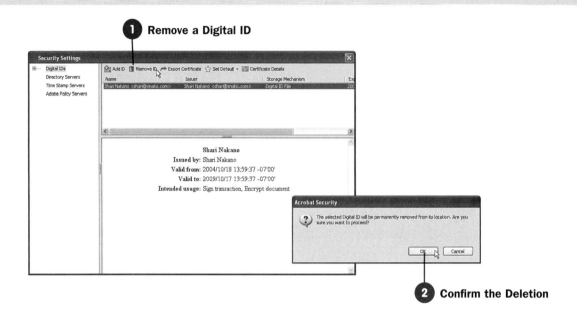

① **Remove a Digital ID**

② **Confirm the Deletion**

---

30 **Add a Digital ID Signature**

Before You Begin

 ✔ **26** Secure a PDF File with Password Protection

See Also

 → **27** Change Security Permissions

Now that you understand digital IDs, you can use a digital ID to apply a signature to your PDF file. By clicking the **Signatures** tab, you can create your own **Signature** field exactly where you want it on the PDF document. Create a blank **Signature** field and then digitally sign the document. If you need multiple signatures, create the blank **Signature** fields first; then send the document to those who you need to digitally sign the PDF document.

① Add a Signature to a PDF

In the **Signatures** tab, select **Create a Blank Signature Field** from the **Options** pop-up menu. Click the **OK** button to accept the instructions; then click and drag in the document window to define the size you want the **Signature** field to be. This launches the **Digital Signature Properties** dialog box. In this dialog box, you can change the look of the **Signature** field.

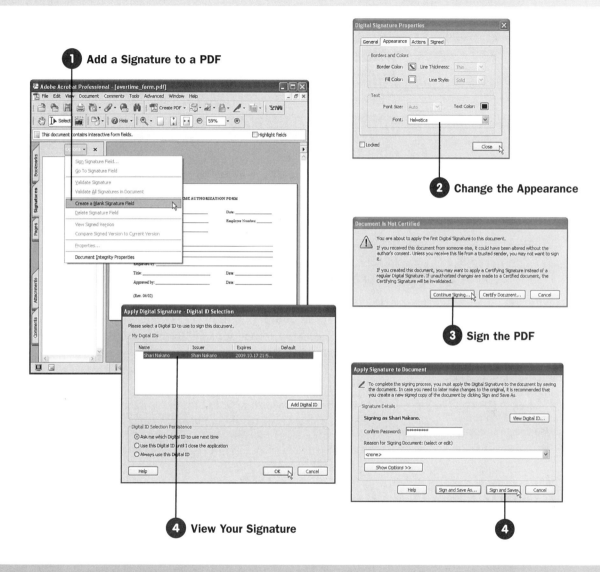

1 Add a Signature to a PDF

2 Change the Appearance

3 Sign the PDF

4 View Your Signature

4

2 Change the Appearance

In the **Digital Signature Properties** dialog box, you can change
how the **Signature** field box looks. Add a colored border or shade
the field altogether. You can also change the font style or color and
specify whether you want the box to perform any actions when it
is clicked.

In the **Signed** tab of the **Digital Signature Properties** dialog box you can select one of the following options: **Nothing Happens When Signed, Mark As Read-only,** or **This Script Executes When Field Is Signed**.

Click the **Close** button when you are satisfied with the looks of your **Signature** field.

3 Sign the PDF

If necessary, click the **Browse** tool to select it and click your new **Signature** field. If the document is not certified, a warning dialog box pops up alerting you of this. Click the **Continue Signing** button to sign the document. The **Apply Digital Signature - Digital ID Selection** dialog box is launched.

4 View Your Signature

TIP

If you always use the same digital ID, select **Always Use This Digital ID** in the **Apply Digital Signature - Digital ID Selection** dialog box. This saves you the step of having to select your digital ID each time you digitally sign a document.

Select the ID with which you want to sign the document and click OK to apply your digital signature. Enter your password for your digital ID. Select your reason for signing the document from the **Reason for Signing Document** pop-up menu. You are required to save the document to complete the process. Either select **Sign and Save** to overwrite the existing document or select **Sign and Save As** to give the document a different name or location. A dialog box appears to let you know the document was successfully signed.

31 Certify a Document

Before You Begin

✔ **26** Secure a PDF File with Password Protection

See Also

➔ **30** Add a Digital ID Signature

By certifying a PDF file, you are ensuring that the file is set up to allow only certain functions and that you are the sole author. This ensures that your information is not changed in any way without your knowledge. After a document is certified, all post-signature changes are listed in the **Signatures** pane. A blue ribbon icon in the **Signatures** pane next to your digital signature indicates that the file is certified. Before certifying a PDF document, make sure you have completed any necessary changes first.

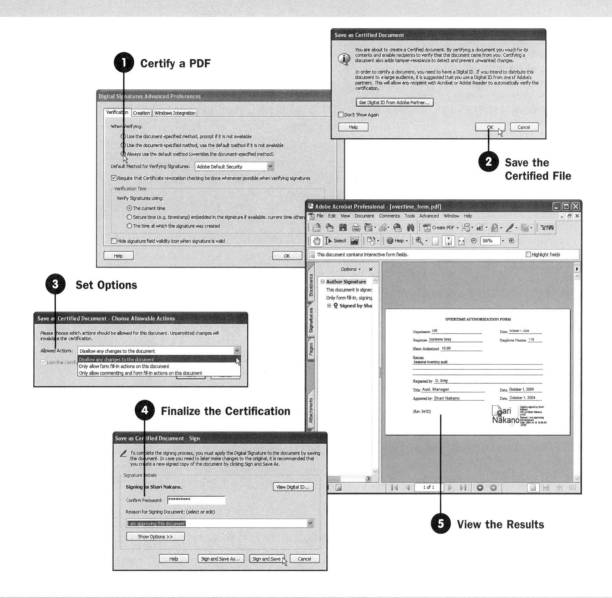

1 Certify a PDF

2 Save the Certified File

3 Set Options

4 Finalize the Certification

5 View the Results

---

1 Certify a PDF

In the **Preferences** dialog box, select the **Security** panel and click the **Advanced Preferences** button. The **Digital Signatures Advanced Preferences** dialog box shows you the preferences available for digital signatures.

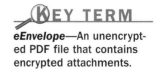

KEY TERM

eEnvelope—An unencrypted PDF file that contains encrypted attachments.

NOTE

In Acrobat 7 eEnvelopes are unencrypted PDF files that contain encrypted attachments. This enables anyone to open and read the PDF file and even view a list of the encrypted attached files, but not open or save the files. You can use an eEnvelope to send Excel spreadsheets with sensitive financial information to your accountant. Your accountant's assistant or colleagues can open the eEnvelope, but only your accountant (to whom you've given the password) can open the spreadsheets. To create an eEnvelope, from the **Document, Security** menu, select **Secure PDF Delivery**. This launches a wizard that walks you through the process of attaching, securing, and delivering the documents.

TIP

When certifying a PDF document, keep in mind both the purpose of the document and the person receiving it. When creating a PDF for the purpose of archiving a document, select **Disallow Any Changes to the Document** from the **Allowed Actions** list to ensure that no one viewing the document can make any changes. When certifying an online form, select **Only Allow Form Fill-in Actions on This Document** from the **Allowed Actions** list so viewers can enter data but not edit the form itself.

If it is not already selected, select **Adobe Default Security** from the **Default Method for Verifying Signatures** pop-up menu. Click **OK**.

2 Save the Certified File

In the **File** menu, select **Save As Certified Document**. This launches the **Save As Certified Document** dialog box. You must have a digital ID to save a document as certified. Click the **OK** button, which launches the **Save As Certified Document—Choose Allowable Actions** dialog box.

3 Set Options

From the **Allowed Actions** pop-up menu choose what you will allow to be done to this particular PDF document. Select from **Disallow Any Changes to the Document, Only Allow Form Fill-in Actions on This Document**, or **Only Allow Commenting and Form Fill-in Actions on This Document**. Click the **Next** button. The warnings are displayed for you to read. Continue to click the **Next** button to finish certifying the document. You can choose either **Show Certification on Document** or **Do Not Show Certification on Document**. If you select the visible certificate, you need to drag a box field onto the document showing where you want the certification to appear.

4 Finalize the Certification

Enter the password for your digital ID in the **Confirm Password** box in the **Save As Certified Document** dialog box; then click the **Sign and Save** button.

5 View the Results

If you chose the **Show Certification on Document** option, the certification shows up on the PDF document, indicated by the digital ID signature and an icon of a document with a blue ribbon attached to it. If you chose the **Do Not Show Certification on Document** option, Acrobat automatically saves the file and the next time the document is opened, a **Document Status** dialog box appears, informing the viewer that the document was certified with a digital signature.

6

Adding Interactivity to a PDF

IN THIS CHAPTER:

Adobe Acrobat provides you with the tools to create a PDF that readers can interact with. Readers can click a link that plays a song or movie, a link to another page in a different PDF, or a link that takes them to a web page on the Internet.

Adding interactivity is a relatively simple process of creating a link that either plays a sound or movie or that performs some other action. These links can be as basic as a navigation link that plays a sound before taking the reader to the next page or as ambitious as an entire multimedia tutorial in a single PDF, with branching lessons based on choices the reader makes.

32 About Interactivity

See Also

→ **33** Create a Multimedia Link

→ **34** Create a Navigation Link

→ **35** Create a Menu Action Link

→ **36** Create a Custom Button

→ **37** Edit a Link

KEY TERMS

Links—Clickable blocks of text or images that perform actions.

Actions—In Acrobat these include displaying specific document location, executing menu commands, playing multimedia files, running JavaScript, etc. The term specifically refers to such actions taken in response to user input, such as clicking a button.

Interactivity is all about allowing the reader to do something with a PDF other than just read it. The primary way to allow the reader to interact with a PDF document is to add *links* to the document. These links can perform various *actions* when clicked, in much the same way that buttons on a website allow the viewer to interact with the website. In fact, the most common types of Acrobat links perform the same functions that most website buttons do—they take the viewer to another page. Navigation links are easy to create and can be extremely useful to the reader, especially in lengthy PDF documents.

In addition to simple navigation links, Acrobat offers 14 other types of links, including everything from submitting forms to executing menu commands. For the record, here are the various actions you can attach to a link and what each one does:

- **Execute a menu item**—Executes any command from any menu in the Acrobat menu bar. This lets you add a lot of functionality to your links, and it's invaluable for full-screen presentations (especially locked, standalone presentations, such as on a trade-show kiosk), where you don't want the Acrobat interface to be displayed.

- **Go to a page view**—Changes the page, magnification level, and page locations displayed in the document window. This is by far the most common action for links.

- **Import form data**—Imports data from an Acrobat PDF (form data file) document and populates existing form fields that exactly match fields in the PDF document.

- **Open a file**—This is pretty self-explanatory. It presents the reader with a standard Open dialog box, within which he can locate and open a document.

- **Open a web link**—Opens a prespecified URL in either Acrobat or the viewer's default browser, depending on how the user's preferences are set.

- **Play a sound**—Plays a prespecified sound file. Acrobat supports most of the standard sound file formats, including WAV, AIFF, and MP3.

- **Play media (Acrobat 5 compatible)**—Plays a linked video file.

- **Play media (Acrobat 6 compatible)**—Plays a video file that can be either linked or embedded in the PDF. The main difference between Acrobat 5 and Acrobat 6 compatibility is Acrobat 6 and 7's capability to embed video files.

- **Read an article**—Takes you to the first page of the specified article and changes your cursor to the Article tool to make it easier to navigate to additional text blocks for the same article.

- **Reset a form**—Removes user data from fields in the current form document. A dialog box allows the user to specify which fields are to be reset.

- **Run a JavaScript**—Runs a block of JavaScript code that you either type or paste into a **JavaScript Editor** dialog box.

- **Set layer visibility**—Lets you display or hide layers that you have defined in the **Layers** pane.

- **Show/hide a field**—Allows the user to show or hide prespecified form fields. This is a great way to create pop-up help text, display conditional fields, and so forth.

- **Submit a form**—Transmits form data from the current document as PDF, XML, or HTML data to a specified URL.

You can have as many links as you want in a PDF file. The links themselves do not increase the file size significantly. You can also have multiple actions in a single link, so that a single link plays a sound, takes the viewer to a new page, plays a short video clip from that page, and then exits out of Acrobat entirely.

One key to making your PDF interactive is to make the interactivity meaningful to the reader. For interactivity to be meaningful, it must enhance either the user's enjoyment or abilities, or both. Adding a sound effect to navigation links just because you can is both pointless and annoying. If, on the other hand, your document uses a theme of some sort and you can add a sound effect that enhances that theme (and doesn't add drastically to the file size), then by all means add the sound effect.

Another key to interactivity is to make the interactive elements of your PDF accessible to the reader. Just because you add some cool interactive element doesn't mean that the reader will know it's there or what it does. Good design and clear, concise text labels or graphical icons can go a long way toward making the interactivity of a PDF document easily accessible to the reader.

33 Create a Multimedia Link

Acrobat allows you to create links in your PDF document that will play sound or movie clips. Readers simply click the link and they can hear a song, listen to voice instructions or view an instructional movie clip. By default, Acrobat embeds the sound or movie clip into the PDF document so you don't have to worry about sending the file along with the PDF to readers, but keep in mind that adding a sound or movie clip can greatly increase the file size of your PDF document (especially movie clips, which can be much larger than sound files).

1 Create a Link

From the **Tools** menu, under the **Advanced Editing** submenu, select the **Link Tool**. While the **Link Tool** is selected, the cursor becomes a cross-hair and any preexisting links become visible.

Press and drag the cross-hairs to create a rectangle at the location you want to create a link. This displays the **Create Link** dialog box, which allows you to change the appearance of a link and its action.

1 **Create a Link**

2 **Select the Link Appearance**

3 **Select the Link Action**

4 **Select the Multimedia File**

2 Select the Link Appearance

The area of a link can be defined by either a visible or an invisible rectangle. This is the area the user can click to activate the link. Obviously, you should have some indicator for the viewer that there is a link he can click, so if you choose an invisible rectangle, make sure there is some graphic or text to indicate a link.

If you choose to make the link visible, select **Visible Rectangle** for **Link Type**. You can then change the rectangle's highlight style, which is a simple change of appearance of the link area, including line thickness, line style, and color, when the viewer clicks it. If you choose to make the link invisible, the **Link Type** needs to be set to **Invisible Rectangle**.

3 Select the Link Action

After you have chosen how you want the link to look, you need to set the link action. In the **Link Action** section, select the **Custom Link** option; then click the **Next** button. Acrobat will bring up the **Link Properties** dialog box. Click the **Actions** tab and select either **Play a Sound** or **Play Media** from the **Select Action** drop-down menu. (There are two **Play Media** options. Select the **Acrobat 5 Compatible** option if you are sending files to users of Acrobat 5; otherwise, select the **Acrobat 6 Compatible** option, which supports a wider variety of video file formats and features.)

3 Select the Multimedia File

After you've clicked the **Add** button, navigate to the movie or sound file you want to add. Select the file. After clicking the **Close** button, press the **Esc** key to return to the normal viewing mode (with the browse tool as the active tool). Click your newly created multimedia link to test it.

TIP

To edit a multimedia link, select the **Link** tool and double-click the link you want to edit. Under the **Actions** section in the **Link Properties** dialog box, select the action and click the **Edit** button. Navigate to the new sound or movie clip and click the **Select** button to change the multimedia file. Click the **Close** button to finish the task.

34 Create a Navigation Link

After creating a PDF document, you might want to include links in the document that take the reader to other pages or to a specific target view to draw attention to a portion of a particular page. To do so, simply create a link that points to that particular page or view.

❶ Create a Link

From the **Tools** menu, under the **Advanced Editing** submenu, select the **Link** tool. If you have the **Advanced Editing** toolbar displayed, click the **Link Tool** button, indicated by the two connecting gold chain links. While the **Link Tool** is selected, the cursor becomes a cross-hair and any preexisting links become visible.

Press and drag the cross-hairs to create a rectangle at the location you want to create a link. This displays the **Create Link** dialog box, which allows you to change the appearance of a link and its action.

❷ Define the Link Appearance

In the **Link Appearance** section in the **Create Link** dialog box, set the **Link Type** to Invisible Rectangle or Visible Rectangle. Then select a Highlight Style of None, Invert, Outline, or Inset. If you are using a visible rectangle, select a Line Thickness of Thin, Medium, or Thick and a Line Style of Solid, Dashed, or Underlined. Then select a line color by clicking the **Color** swatch and selecting a color from the pop-up palette.

❸ Set the Destination

After you have chosen how you want the link to look, you must set the link action. Under the **Link Action** section, select the **Go to a Page View** option; then click the **Next** button. When the **Create Go to View** dialog box appears, set the link's destination by navigating to the target page and, if desired, changing the magnification and page location. Then click the **Set Link** button.

Before You Begin

✔ **32** About Interactivity

See Also

→ **37** Edit a Link

 TIP

To create a navigation link between two documents, go through the steps described in this task, but when the **Create Go to View** dialog box appears, don't navigate to another page in the current document. Instead, use the **Open** command in the **File** menu to open a second document and navigate to the page, magnification level, and page location you want; then click the **Set Link** button. This creates a link in the original document that takes the viewer to a location in the second document.

When linking to another PDF document, it is important to remember that the readers must have access to all the linked documents; otherwise, they will be unable to view the linked PDF. Be sure to include all the files and folders for a PDF when sending it to readers.

You can also set a link to open another file, not just link to another page in a different PDF document. When creating a link, in the **Create Link** dialog box under the **Link Action** section, select the **Open a File** option. Navigate to the file you want Acrobat to open when the reader clicks the link.

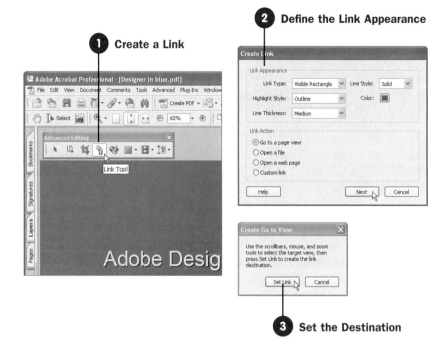

① Create a Link

② Define the Link Appearance

③ Set the Destination

35 Create a Menu Action Link

Before You Begin

✔ **32** About Interactivity

See Also

→ **37** Edit a Link

The **Execute** menu item link actions let you create links that allow the reader of a PDF document to execute virtually any menu command in Acrobat with the click of a button. You can even create links that execute multiple menu items. Probably the best use of this feature is to provide an easy way to work with the document for readers who either are unfamiliar with Acrobat or have limited menu access (due to either document settings or visual/motion impairments).

For example, if you are designing a stand alone presentation kiosk for a trade show, you will want to hide the interface from the user so they cannot exit the application or alter it in any way. The main menu of the presentation would contain links to open other PDF presentations. Those presentations would each contain a link to execute the File, Close menu item. This would exit the secondary presentation and return the user back to the main presentation.

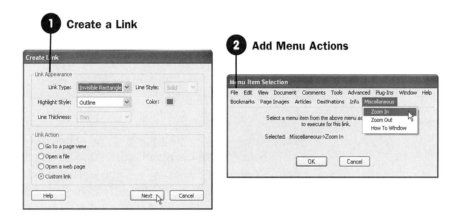

1 Create a Link

2 Add Menu Actions

Because you can never know how proficient the user may or may not be with Acrobat, you can use links to ensure that users have access to Acrobat features that you want them to use. For example, in a PDF document intended for users who may have visual impairments, placing a large link that executes the View, Read Out Loud command can be very helpful. In a document that is intended to be used as a reference, placing a link that executes the Edit, Find command can also be helpful.

1 Create a Link

Click the **Link Tool** button on the **Advanced Editing** toolbar. Click and drag the cross-hairs to create a rectangular link box on the location you want to create the link. This brings up the **Create Link** dialog box.

Set the appearance of the rectangular link box by changing the link type, highlight style, line thickness, style, and color in the **Link Appearance** section of the **Create Link** dialog box. If you choose the invisible rectangle link type, be sure to provide an obvious visual cue to let the viewer know that there is an available link for her to click.

For example, by making the text blue and underlined, like a hyperlink or by placing the invisible link over an obvious button graphic.

❷ Add Menu Actions

In the **Link Action** section, click the **Custom Link** option and then click the **Next** button. Acrobat displays the **Actions** tab of the **Link Properties** dialog box. In the **Add an Action** section, select **Execute a Menu Item** from the **Select Action** drop-down list; then click the **Add** button.

If you are on a Windows computer, a dialog box appears that contains all the menus in the menu bar. Click a menu and select the command you want the link to execute when clicked. The selected command is listed just above the **OK** button. Click the **OK** button and the action is added to the list of actions for this link. If you want to add more menu commands, just select **Execute a Menu Item** from the **Select Action** drop-down list again, click the **Add** button, and select another menu command from the dialog box that appears.

If you are on a Macintosh computer, a dialog box appears prompting you to select the desired command from the actual menus in the menu bar. The command does not execute when selected; instead, it is listed in the dialog box and is added to the link actions list when you click the **OK** button. (For reasons that are too technical to get into in a book about Acrobat, Windows programmers have to fake all the menus and menu commands in the dialog box, but Macintosh programmers can just have the dialog box intercept and remember which command you select from the real menus without the application actually performing the command.)

Click the **Close** button at the bottom of the **Link Properties** dialog box to finish creating your link. Select the **Browse** tool in the toolbar (or just press the **Esc** key) and click the link to test it. It should execute the menu command (or commands) just as if you had selected it from the menu yourself.

36 Create a Custom Button

In addition to creating links, Acrobat also gives you the ability to create either text-based or custom graphical buttons. Both buttons and links perform actions, but the advantage of buttons is that they look like buttons. That is to say, they appear on your document as familiar and obviously clickable elements instead of invisible rectangles or rectangles whose meanings might be unclear. Obviously, if your PDF document already contains obvious cues, an invisible or visible link rectangle placed over the cue will get the job done. But if you are adding functionality that wasn't planned when the source document was created and converted, buttons can let the viewer know what to click and why.

1 Create a PDF Icon and Create a Button

If all you want is a text-based button, you can skip this step. But if you want an icon of some sort for your button, you need to create it first. Acrobat does not come with any button graphics.

To create a PDF icon, exit or minimize Acrobat and either locate a small image to use as your icon or create one in Photoshop, Illustrator, or any number of other graphics applications. When you have a small image, create a PDF version of it by printing it to PDF (see **5** **About Creating a PDF from Other Applications**) or by converting the file within Acrobat (see **1** **Create a PDF in Acrobat**). However you do it, you need to end up with a PDF version of a small, icon-size image.

From the **Tools** menu, select the **Advanced Editing** submenu and the **Button** tool. Double-click or click and drag with the crosshair cursor where you want the button to appear. Acrobat presents you with the **Button Properties** dialog box.

2 Define the Button Appearance

Click the **General** tab, if it does not come up by default, and enter a name for the button in the **Name** field. In the **Tooltip** field, type in a short description of what the button does. This ToolTip appears when the viewer holds the mouse cursor over the button, just like the ToolTips for the buttons in the toolbars. If you are not using a custom icon, you might want to change some of the settings in the **Appearance** tab, but for a custom graphical button, this isn't necessary.

Before You Begin

✔ **33** Create a Multimedia Link

See Also

→ **34** Create a Navigation Link

→ **35** Create a Menu Action Link

→ **37** Edit a Link

💡 TIP

If you own Illustrator, you already have a large selection of images that are perfect for use as icons. The brushes and symbols that come with Illustrator can be used royalty-free for any purpose you desire (assuming you legally own your copy of Illustrator, of course). Many other graphics applications also come with clip art or other images you can use for your own purposes. While Photoshop doesn't come with a library of image objects like Illustrator, Photoshop's layer effects, such as drop shadow and bevels, are ideal for creating your own custom button graphics.

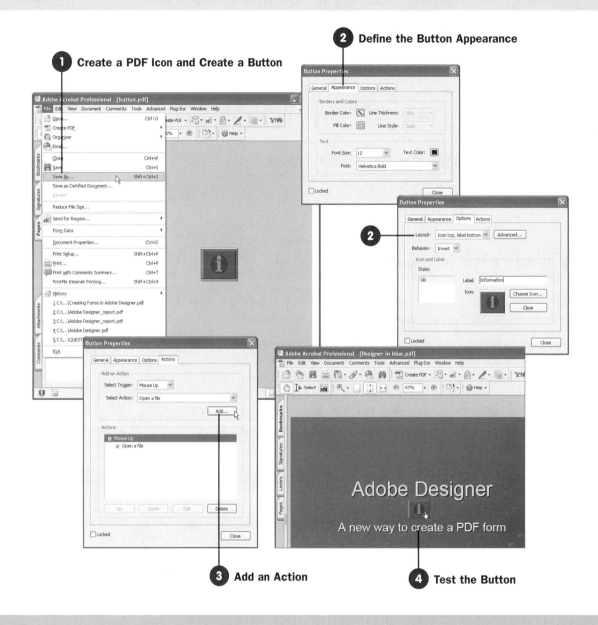

2 Define the Button Appearance

1 Create a PDF Icon and Create a Button

3 Add an Action

4 Test the Button

Click the **Options** tab. From the **Layout** drop-down list, select which combination of icon and/or label you want to use for your button. Click the **Choose Icon** button on the right side of the dialog box and locate and open the PDF icon file you created earlier.

3 Add an Action

Click the **Actions** tab. Select an action from the **Select Action** drop-down list. You can also choose a trigger (the mouse action that triggers the selected action), but you will probably want to stick with the default, **Mouse Up**. This means that the action does not take place until the viewer releases the mouse button as the second half of a click of the button.

Define whatever parameters are necessary for your action, such as navigating to a specific page, selecting a sound or video file, or choosing a menu command to execute.

Click the **Close** button to exit the dialog box and complete the button-creation process.

4 Test the Button

Now it's time to test the button. To exit the **Button Tool** mode, press the **Esc** button. This returns you to the normal viewing mode with the **Browse** tool as the active tool. Click the newly created button to test it.

37 Edit a Link

When making changes to a PDF document, you might also need to change the links within the document. A link to a particular page view might now be pointing to an incorrect page, or you might decide to change the action completely.

1 Select a Link

Click the **Link Tool** button the **Advanced Editing** toolbar to display all the available links in your document. Double-click the link you want to change. This opens the **Link Properties** dialog box.

2 Change the Appearance

Click the **Appearance** tab to change the appearance of your link, such as making it visible or invisible. You can also change the **Highlight Style** to **None, Invert, Outside,** or **Inset**. You can also change the thickness of a line, its line style, and its color.

Before You Begin

✔ **33** Create a Multimedia Link

✔ **34** Create a Navigation Link

✔ **35** Create a Menu Action Link

✔ **36** Create a Custom Button

2 Change the Appearance

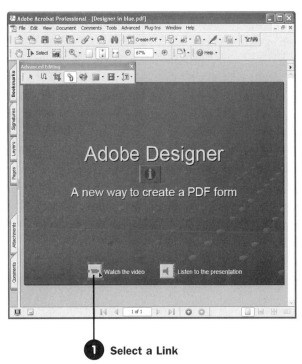

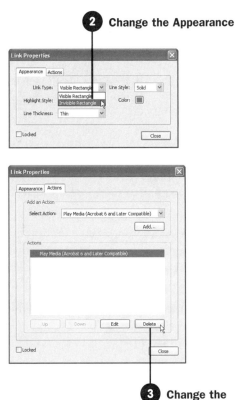

1 Select a Link

3 Change the
Action

NOTE

Editing a button is just as
easy as editing a link.
Simply select the **Button**
tool instead of the **Link**
tool; double-click the button; and change the set-
tings in the **General**,
Appearance, **Options**, and
Actions tabs.

3 **Change the Action**

In the **Link Properties** dialog box, click the **Actions** tab. Select the
action in the **Actions** section; then click the **Delete** button. This
removes the current action associated with the link so you can add
a new action. Select a new action from the drop-down box located
in the **Add an Action** section.

7

Creating a PDF Presentation

IN THIS CHAPTER:

TIP

If you are creating a PDF version of a PowerPoint slideshow, you can save yourself some work by selecting the **Change Conversion Settings** command in the **Adobe PDF** menu in PowerPoint and selecting the **Save Slide Transitions in Adobe PDF**, **Save Animations in Adobe PDF** (if you are using slide animations), and **Convert Multimedia to PDF Multimedia** (if you are incorporating multimedia) options.

Acrobat's capability to convert almost any document into PDF format and then display that PDF file in a full-screen mode opens a whole new set of opportunities for creating compelling onscreen presentations. No longer are you limited to presentations that consist of nothing but one slide after another. Use Acrobat to quickly and easily convert a business plan into a presentation; to display a collection of family vacation photos; or to create a full-screen slideshow-style presentation from virtually any document or collection of documents, including photographs, audio, and video.

The key to a nice presentation is to ensure each page is of the same size and resolution. Use a program such as InDesign to get the pages a consistent size, and then use Acrobat's **Create PDF from Multiple Files** feature to bring all the pages into one document. When all your pages are collected, you can use a variety of transition effects to add visual interest or use the same effect for each page if consistency is what you want.

38 View a PDF in Full Screen View

See Also

→ **2** Create a PDF from Multiple Files

→ **4** Create PDFs from Microsoft Office

TIP

A new feature added to Acrobat 7 is a full-screen toggle icon located in the bottom-left corner of the document window. Click the icon to view the PDF presentation in full screen mode. To exit full screen mode and return to the regular viewing mode, either press (⌘-L) [Ctrl+L] or press the **Esc** key.

Full Screen mode displays a PDF file on a black background with only the document showing. That means no windows, menus, or floating palettes appear, just the document as you would see it as a slide. In addition to presentations, you can use **Full Screen** mode to see how your PDF will look when printed or used as a web page with no distracting menus or palettes.

1 **Enter Full Screen Mode**

From the **Window** menu or the **View** menu (the command appears in both menus), select the **Full Screen** command. You can also use the (⌘-L) [**Ctrl+L**] keyboard shortcut. Acrobat hides the application interface and displays the document only, set against a black background.

2 **View the Presentation**

Use the **right arrow**, **down arrow**, or **Page Down** key to advance from one page/slide to the next. Use the **left arrow**, **up arrow**, or **Page Up** key to return to the previous slide. You can also left-click to advance to the next slide and right-click (Windows) or **Ctrl**-click (Mac OS) to return to the previous slide.

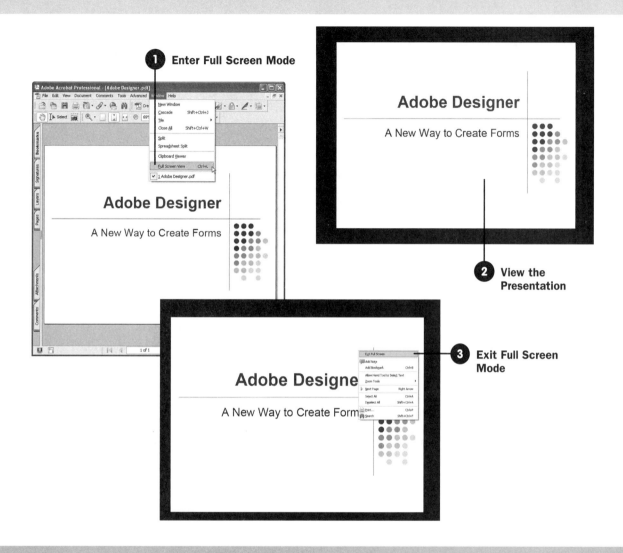

Enter Full Screen Mode

View the Presentation

Exit Full Screen Mode

③ Exit Full Screen Mode

Press the **Esc** key to exit **Full Screen** mode and return to the normal Acrobat interface. You can also exit the full screen mode by left-clicking to bring up a menu. Click **Exit Full Screen** to exit back to Acrobat.

39 Incorporate Multimedia in a Presentation

Before You Begin

✔ **33** Create a Multimedia Link

Adding *multimedia* to a PDF can be accomplished with a few simple clicks and drags of the mouse. All you need to do is select the **Add Sound** or **Add Movie** tool, create a link, and specify a source file and a few options. Adding sound or video to a PDF file is a great way to add some pizzazz to a presentation or make a document come alive.

One important caveat to keep in mind is that adding sound or video can greatly increase the size of the PDF file (especially for video) if you choose to embed the multimedia files. You do not have to embed the multimedia source files into the PDF, but if you don't, you must ensure that the multimedia files are delivered along with the PDF and that their location remains the same relative to the PDF file that links to them (such as keeping them all in the same folder).

KEY TERM

Multimedia—This refers to digital content other than text or static graphics, including audio, video, and animation.

NOTE

The point of a *poster* is to provide the user with some idea of the content of the movie. If your movie fades in from black (as many do) or has an initial frame that doesn't convey meaningful information about the movie clip itself, the default option of using the first frame of the movie isn't very helpful and should be avoided. Instead, consider creating a file based on a different frame in the movie or a piece of concept art and using that as the poster for your movie.

KEY TERM

Poster—A still image used to represent the content of a video clip. It is often the first frame of the video, but it can also be a piece of concept art.

① Create a Multimedia Link

Click the **Tools** menu, select the **Advanced Editing** submenu, and select **Movie Tool** or **Sound Tool**. Click and drag (or simply double-click) with either tool in your document to define a size and location for the hot spot for the link. This launches the **Add Sound** or **Add Movie** dialog box.

② Specify a Source File

Click the **Browse** button and locate and open the desired sound or movie file on your hard drive. For movie files, make sure the **Snap to Content Proportions** check box is selected. For both sound and movie files, make sure the **Embed Content in Document** check box is selected if you want to embed the source files in the PDF.

The **Poster Settings** section lets you set the initial image for the link. For movie links, the default option is to create the poster from the movie (using the first frame of the movie), although you can choose to not use a poster or to create a poster from a file. For sound links, your only choices are to not use a poster or to create a poster from a file.

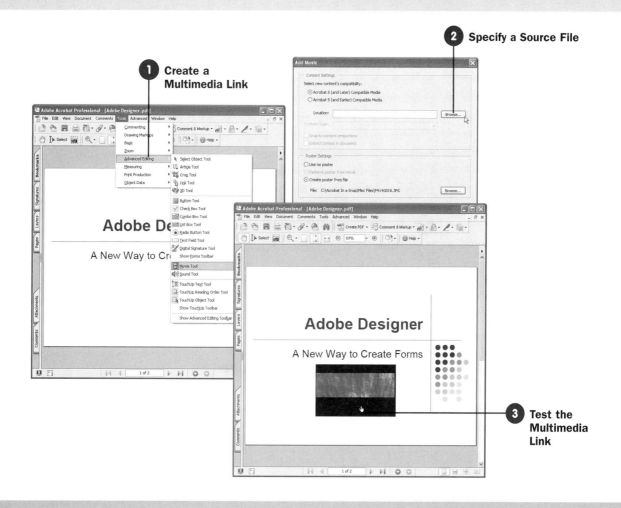

2 Specify a Source File

1 Create a Multimedia Link

3 Test the Multimedia Link

---

3 **Test the Multimedia Link**

Using the **Hand** tool, click the multimedia link you just created. Your sound or movie will start playing. You can rewind and fast forward movies while they play with the left and right arrow keys; however, you can't stop the sound from playing after you activate it.

 TIP

Change the look of the sound button by right-clicking (Windows) or Ctrl-clicking (Mac OS) the sound link and selecting **Properties**. In the **Multimedia Properties** dialog box, click the **Appearance** tab and change the border color, outline, or style.

40 Set Presentation Preferences

Before You Begin

✔ **2** View a PDF in Full Screen View

See Also

→ **41** Include Page Transitions

Now that you can view the **Full Screen** mode for a presentation, you can alter how the slideshow is viewed. The default background is black for the slides. If you are looking for a punch of color, select a colored background. Make sure it looks good with all the slides, though. Set the slides to automatically advance, and set the time between slides. This is perfect if you are speaking along with the slideshow. Practice and see how long your explanation runs, and have the automatic advance follow your time.

1 Change Background Color

From the **Edit** menu, select the **Preferences** command. In the **Preferences** dialog box, select **Full Screen** from the list of options along the left side. Click the black **Background Color** swatch, and then select either a preset color or the **Other** swatch to activate the **Colors** dialog box. In the **Colors** dialog box, select a new color and click the **OK** button.

2 Set Navigation Preferences

If you want your presentation to automatically advance, select the **Advance Every _ Seconds** check box. Enter the amount of time you want each slide to stay onscreen. If you want the presentation to continually run, select the **Loop After Last Page** check box. If you want onscreen navigation buttons, select the **Show Navigation Bar** check box.

If you want the **Esc** key to enable you to exit your presentation, check the **Escape Key Exits** box. Another option is to set that the left-click of your mouse will advance the slide presentation forward and that a right-click will advance the presentation backward.

TIP

If you are speaking along with the presentation, you might want to chose the left-click/right-click navigation option in the **Full Screen Preferences** window. With this option selected and a wireless mouse, you can advance slides from just about anywhere in the room (depending on the size of the room, of course).

3 View the Presentation

Click the **OK** button to close the **Preferences** dialog box. To view the presentation in full screen mode, select the **Full Screen** command from either the **View** or **Window** menu, or click the **Full Screen View** toggle icon in the lower-left corner and advance through your slides to see your presentation with the new settings. To exit full screen mode and return to the regular viewing mode, press **Esc**.

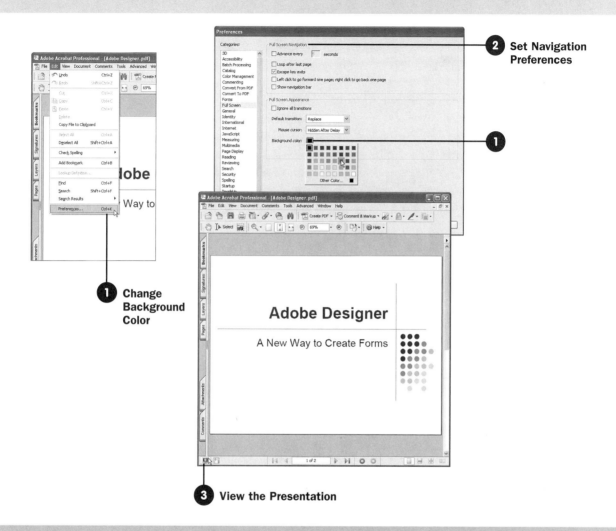

2 Set Navigation Preferences

1

1 Change Background Color

3 View the Presentation

41 Include Page Transitions

Page transitions are what you see when one slide advances to the next slide. You can choose from a variety of default transitions for the entire presentation, use random transitions, or set specific transitions between pages. If you want the whole presentation to have the same transition, you can set that in **Full Screen Preferences** or in the **Document** menu with **Set Page Transitions**. Try the various transitions and then pick the one that works best with the information and visuals in your presentation.

Before You Begin

✔ **40** Set Presentation Preferences

See Also

→ **38** View a PDF in Full Screen View

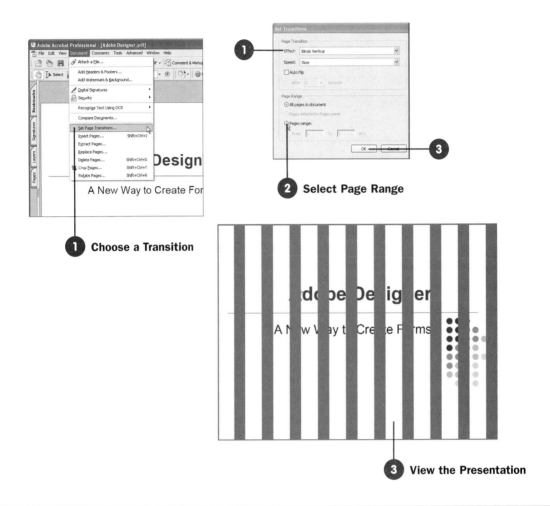

1 Choose a Transition

2 Select Page Range

3 View the Presentation

1 Choose a Transition

From the **Document** menu, select the **Set Page Transitions** command. In the **Page Transition** section of the **Set Transitions** dialog box, select one of the 40 available transitions from the **Effect** drop-down list. Then select a transition speed (slow, medium, or fast) from the **Speed** drop-down list. If you want your slides to advance automatically, select the **Auto Flip** option.

2 **Select Page Range**

In the **Page Range** section, specify to which pages/slides you want these transitions applied. You can select from either **All Pages in Document** or **Pages Selected in Pages Panel** (available only if you have the **Pages** panel open), or you can specify a range of pages.

3 **View the Presentation**

Click the **OK** button to close the **Set Transitions** dialog box; then select the **Full Screen** command from either the **Window** or **View** menu. View the presentation a couple of times, noting which transitions look right and which ones need to be changed. Then return to the **Set Transitions** dialog box and make any necessary changes.

TIP

Select a transition that doesn't detract from the primary focus of your presentation, which is the information you are trying to convey. Acrobat provides many stylish transition effects. Select the one that fits the overall tone of your presentation.

8

Creating Bookmarks

IN THIS CHAPTER:

KEY TERMS

Bookmark—A special type of navigation link that appears in the Bookmarks panel of the navigation pane, rather than in the document itself.

Links—In Acrobat, these are clickable areas that perform an action. The most common types of links are navigation links, which take you to a new location. However, links can also run JavaScript, execute menu items, play sounds or video, and so on.

A *bookmark* is a navigation link to a specific location in a PDF file. A bookmark can link to an entire page, a specific block of text, an image, or anything in between. You set the destination (including the page, location, and magnification level) when you create the bookmark. Bookmarks usually link to a location in the same document, but they can link to other documents as well.

Unlike other types of *links*, bookmarks do not appear in the document itself. Instead, they are displayed as a list in the **Bookmarks** panel of the **Navigation** pane. By displaying all the bookmarks together in one place, Acrobat allows the reader to get an overview of the document and to easily navigate to a specific section or entry. This is especially useful in lengthy or complex documents. The **Bookmarks** panel can be opened or closed by clicking the **Bookmarks** tab along the left side of the document window.

Because a bookmark is simply a special type of link, you can change or add actions to a bookmark in the same way you can to any link, as described in **35** **Create a Menu Action Link**. This enables you to create bookmarks that link to websites, play multimedia clips, or submit form data, in addition to serving as navigational aids.

42 Create a Bookmark

See Also

→ **43** Change a Bookmark's Destination

→ **46** Organize Bookmarks

Bookmarks are almost as easy to create as they are to use. The **Bookmarks** panel contains buttons for creating and deleting bookmarks, as well as an **Options** menu with additional bookmark-related commands.

When creating bookmarks, the most important thing to keep in mind is that the default destination for a newly created bookmark is whatever is displayed in the document pane. For this reason, it's important that you define where the bookmark will go *before* you create the bookmark. This might seem backwards at first, but it makes bookmark creation fast and easy, as you will see.

1 Open the Bookmarks Panel

If necessary, click the **Bookmarks** tab (on the left side of the Acrobat document window) to display the **Bookmarks** panel.

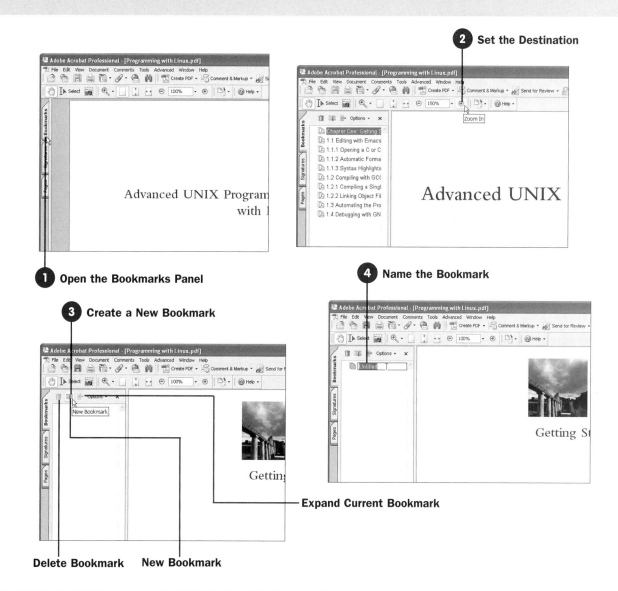

2 Set the Destination

1 Open the Bookmarks Panel

3 Create a New Bookmark

4 Name the Bookmark

Expand Current Bookmark

Delete Bookmark   New Bookmark

2 Set the Destination

Go to the page, location, and magnification that you want your new bookmark to point to. Whatever is displayed in the document pane when creating the bookmark is exactly what is displayed when the bookmark is used.

TIPS

You can also use the keyboard shortcut **Ctrl+B** (Windows) or ⌘-**B** (Mac OS) to create a new bookmark.

If you highlight a block of text in your document before creating the bookmark, the highlighted text is used as the name of the new bookmark.

NOTE

After it's created, a bookmark can easily be renamed or deleted by right-clicking (Windows) or **Ctrl**-clicking (Mac OS) on the bookmark and selecting either the **Rename** or **Delete** command from the context menu.

For example, if you want the bookmark you are creating to take the reader to a sidebar on page 17 of your document, navigate in the file to page 17, change the magnification level to 200% (or whatever magnification level is appropriate to the size of the sidebar), and scroll the page so the sidebar is displayed in the document pane.

3 Create a New Bookmark

Click the **New Bookmark** icon at the top of the **Bookmarks** panel, or click the **Options** button on the **Bookmarks** panel and select the **New Bookmark** command.

4 Name the Bookmark

The default name of the new bookmark (Untitled) is automatically highlighted by Acrobat in the **Bookmarks** pane. Simply type in a new name and press **Enter**.

43 Change a Bookmark's Destination

See Also

→ **44** Create a Bookmark to a Different Document

As you make changes to a PDF file, you might find that an existing bookmark no longer points to the correct location. Or you might simply have made a mistake when creating a bookmark in the first place. In either case, it is far easier to point an existing bookmark to a new location than to delete the bookmark and create a new one. Changing a bookmark's destination is a simple matter of navigating to the correct destination and resetting the bookmark to point to this new location.

1 Navigate to a New Destination

In the document pane, go to the page, magnification level, and page location to which you want this bookmark to point. If you want the bookmark to point to an entire page, go to that page and set the magnification to **Fit Page**. If you want the bookmark to point to a magnified version of a graphic, go to the appropriate page, increase the magnification level, and scroll the page to center the graphic in the document pane.

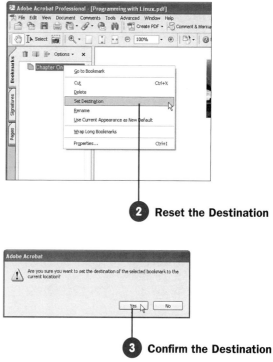

① Navigate to a
New Destination

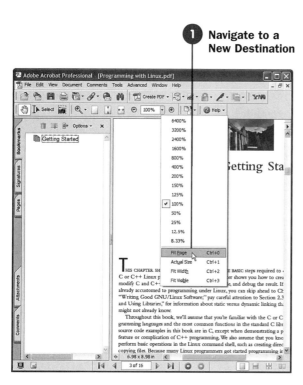

② Reset the Destination

③ Confirm the Destination

② Reset the Destination

Right-click (Windows) or **Ctrl**-click (Mac OS) the bookmark whose
destination you want to change; then select **Set Destination** from
the context menu.

③ Confirm the Destination

Click the **Yes** button in the confirmation dialog box. The bookmark now points to the destination displayed in the document
pane. To test this, navigate to a different page, magnification level,
and page location and then click the bookmark you just created to
confirm that it works as intended.

44 Create a Bookmark to a Different Document

Before You Begin

✔ **42** Create a Bookmark

 TIP

Planning a multiple-document PDF presentation is a lot like planning a website. You need to use good design to let the viewer know where he is in the presentation. This can be done with titles or sidebar text, or graphically using different background colors, logos, or other visual cues.

Bookmarks are not limited to use only as navigational tools within a single document. A bookmark can point to a specific location in any document to which you (and whoever will eventually be viewing the files) has access. Creating cross-document bookmarks isn't as simple or as intuitive as creating regular bookmarks, but if you follow the steps in this task, you'll see that it's a relatively quick and painless process.

One thing to keep in mind with cross-document bookmarks is that the viewer might not have any idea that the bookmark has taken him to another document. The only indication Acrobat provides is the document name in the application window title bar. It's always a good idea to let the viewer know he is in another document and to provide a way for him to get back to the original document, such as a **Return to Main Menu** bookmark in each destination document.

Another important consideration is that the viewer must have access to all the documents and that the organization structure of the documents must remain intact. For example, you might create a folder called **Product Demo** and in that folder put the main document (called **Start Here** or something similar), as well as subfolders for different PDFs used in the demo (called **At Work**, **At School**, and **At Play**, for example). For someone else to go through the demo and access all the files, you need to give them the entire **Product Demo** folder with all its files and subfolders intact. This is how many tech support documentation CDs are arranged. Having one big PDF file with all the pages in it is definitely easier, but breaking the information into separate files lets you replace parts of the presentation without affecting everything else.

① Create a New Bookmark

Click the **New Bookmark** icon at the top of the **Bookmarks** tab.

It doesn't matter what is displayed in the document window because you'll be changing this bookmark's destination in the next steps.

② View the Bookmark's Action Properties

Right-click (Windows) or **Ctrl**-click (Mac OS) the bookmark and select **Properties** from the drop-down menu; then click the **Actions** tab in the **Properties** dialog box.

1 Create a New Bookmark

2 View the Bookmark's Action Properties

4 Add a New Action

3 Delete the Current Action

6 Create the Link

5 Navigate to a New Destination

3 Delete the Current Action

The default action for all bookmarks is a **Go to a Page in This Document** action that points to whatever was displayed in the document pane at the time the bookmark was created. You need to delete this action so you can replace it with an action that points to a location in a different document. Furthermore, you cannot simply reset the bookmark's destination (as described in **43** **Change a Bookmark's Destination**) because that command doesn't give you the opportunity to specify a different document as the destination.

Select **Go to a Page in This Document** in the **Actions** list, and click the **Delete** button.

4 Add a New Action

From the **Select Action** drop-down list, select **Go to a Page View** and click the **Add** button.

After you add the **Go to a Page View** action, Acrobat allows you to set the destination by navigating to the page to which you want the action to take you. This is the key to creating a link to another document. You are not limited to choosing a page from the current document. Until you click the **Set Link** button in the **Create Go to View** dialog box, you can open, close, and navigate in as many different documents as you need to until you find the exact page you are looking for.

5 Navigate to a New Destination

With the **Create Go to View** dialog box onscreen, open another PDF file and navigate to the desired page, magnification, and location.

Remember that, for the viewer to be able to use this link, he needs both the main document and any destination documents—and these documents need to be kept in the same hierarchical folder structure relative to each other that they were in when the link was created.

6 Create the Link

Click the **Set Link** button in the **Create Go to View** dialog box. The bookmark in the original document is now linked to the second document you specified in step 5.

TIP

Even though bookmarks are created, displayed, and used in a separate panel, they are basically just another type of link. As such, a bookmark can perform any action you would normally associate with a link, such as playing sounds, performing menu commands, or displaying or resetting forms or fields. Keep in mind that most viewers of PDF documents have an expectation of what will happen when they click a bookmark, so be sure to exercise discretion when using bookmarks to perform non-navigation actions.

45 Generate Bookmarks from Structured Documents

One little-known but extremely useful feature of Acrobat is its capability to automatically generate bookmarks from structured PDF files. Of course, using this feature requires an understanding of what a structured PDF file is.

A *structured PDF file* contains internal *tags* that describe the nature of the elements within the file. These tags are used most often to make a file more accessible to those with motion or vision disabilities. Structured PDF files can also be viewed more easily on different devices, such as PDAs and cell phones. Structured PDF files can be created from many authoring applications, such as Adobe InDesign and Microsoft Word (especially if you use styles in your Word document). For more information on structured and tagged PDF files and how to create them, see **60** **Create an Accessible PDF**.

The information stored in structured PDF files can also be used as the basis for automatically generating bookmarks. Bookmarks created this way are *structured bookmarks*, not regular bookmarks. The key difference between the two is that regular bookmarks contain navigation links that take the viewer to a particular page and location but they are not tied to the destination in any way. You can move or delete a regular bookmark without affecting the page it points to. Structured bookmarks, on the other hand, are linked to the pages they point to. Moving or deleting a structured bookmark moves or deletes the page to which it points.

❶ Open a Structured PDF File

All MS Word and InDesign files have the necessary structural information, as does any file specifically saved as a structured file in an authoring program that supports structured files, such as Adobe FrameMaker. Aside from MS Word and InDesign files, there is no way to know whether a document is a structured file except to open it in its original authoring application and check (using whatever method that authoring program uses to display structural information).

Before You Begin

✔ **4** Create PDFs from Microsoft Office

See Also

➜ **46** Organize Bookmarks

➜ **60** Create an Accessible PDF

 KEY TERMS

Structured PDF—These files contain additional information about the various elements (images, blocks of text, and so forth) in the PDF file. This structure improves the reflow of the document on handheld devices and is used by accessibility technology for viewers with vision or motion impairments.

Tags—Invisible (to us) blocks of information about each individual document element in a PDF file.

Structured bookmark—A bookmark that is tied to its destination page so that moving or deleting the bookmark also moves or deletes the destination page. Structured bookmarks can be created only in structured PDF files because the relationship between the structured bookmark and destination page is based on the logical structure tree found in structured PDF files.

1 **Open a Structured PDF File**

2 **Create New Bookmarks from Structure**

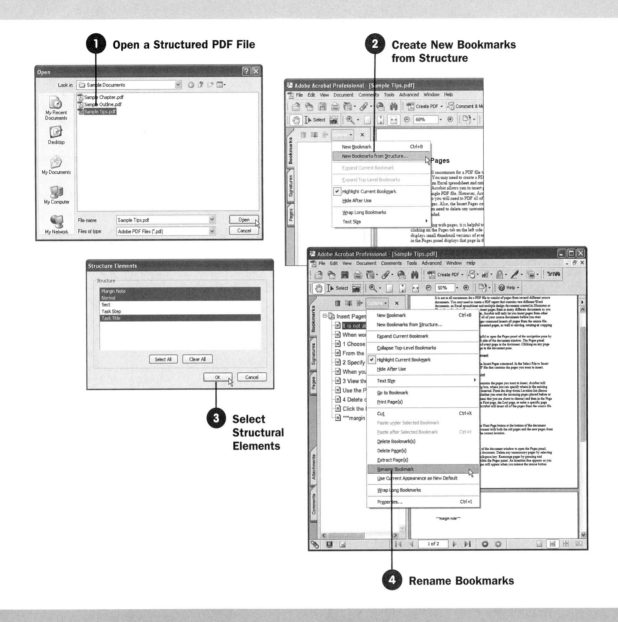

3 **Select Structural Elements**

4 **Rename Bookmarks**

2 **Create New Bookmarks from Structure**

Open the **Bookmarks** panel, if necessary; then click the **Options** button and select **New Bookmarks from Structure**. The **Structure Elements** dialog box opens.

③ Select Structural Elements

In the **Structure Elements** dialog box, click the structural elements you want to use as the basis for your bookmarks. **Ctrl**-click (Windows) or ⌘-click (Mac OS) to select multiple elements. Click the **OK** button to generate the bookmarks.

Typically, the structural elements that make the most sense to use as the basis for bookmarks are paragraph styles. Typically, bookmarks are generated from the styles used for chapter and section headings. In addition to styles, many structured documents contain structural data or tags for tables, images, and paragraph or column breaks that would be inappropriate to use to create bookmarks.

④ Rename Bookmarks

Click the plus symbol next to the bookmark icons to expand heading bookmarks and select the bookmark. Click the **Options** button and select **Rename**. Type in the new name of the bookmark and press **Enter** to accept the changes.

46 Organize Bookmarks

The more bookmarks you have in your document, the more important it is to organize them into a logical and easy-to-use structure. This can be as simple as changing the order in which the bookmarks are listed or as ambitious as creating a hierarchical structure that includes main heading, subheading, and even tertiary bookmarks (although more than two levels of bookmarks is generally not recommended).

Bookmarks can be rearranged by simply dragging the bookmark up or down in the bookmark list. The key thing to pay attention to when moving bookmarks is the location of the insertion point in the bookmark list (shown as an arrowhead and dotted line). If the insertion point is below the icon of another bookmark, the bookmark being dragged is placed below the target at the same level in the hierarchy. If the insertion point is below the name of another bookmark, the bookmark being dragged is placed below the target and subordinate to the target in the hierarchy.

Before You Begin

✔ **42** Create a Bookmark

✔ **43** Change a Bookmark's Destination

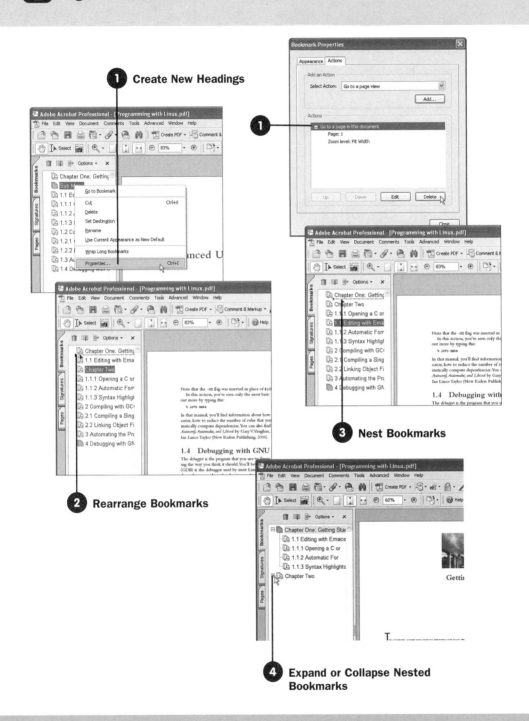

1 Create New Headings

2 Rearrange Bookmarks

3 Nest Bookmarks

4 Expand or Collapse Nested Bookmarks

❶ Create New Headings

To help you organize your bookmarks into logical groups, you might want to create some empty bookmarks that don't do anything other than act as headings for your other bookmarks. To do this, create a bookmark and give it an appropriate heading name. Right-click (Windows) or **Ctrl**-click (Mac OS) the bookmark and select **Properties** from the context menu. In the **Properties** dialog box, click the **Actions** tab, select the **Go to a Page in This Document** action in the **Actions** list, and click the **Delete** button. Click **Close**, and the new bookmark will have no action. That is, it will be only a heading in your list of bookmarks.

❷ Rearrange Bookmarks

Position the mouse pointer over the icon for the bookmark you want to move, and then drag the icon up or down until the insertion point (the arrow and dotted line) is under the icon of another bookmark; then release the mouse button. You have successfully moved one bookmark in the list so it has the same level in the hierarchy as the bookmark immediately above it in the list.

❸ Nest Bookmarks

Position the mouse pointer over the icon for the bookmark you want to move, and drag the icon up or down until the insertion point is under the name of another bookmark; then release the mouse button. After bookmarks are nested, headings can be expanded or collapsed by clicking the plus or minus icon next to the bookmark. You have successfully moved one bookmark in the list so it is subordinate to (nested under) the bookmark immediately above it in the list.

The top-level bookmark in a set of nested bookmarks is provided with an icon you can click to expand or collapse the list of nested bookmarks.

❹ Expand or Collapse Nested Bookmarks

Click the plus-sign icon (Windows) or the reveal triangle (Mac OS) next to the topmost heading to expand the list of bookmarks. Click the minus-sign icon (Windows) or the reveal triangle again (Mac OS) to collapse the list.

PART III

Taking It
Up a Notch

IN THIS PART:

9

Working with Forms in Adobe Designer

IN THIS CHAPTER:

In this chapter, you learn how to create a PDF form both in Acrobat and in Adobe Designer, Adobe's new form creating application. Designer ships free of charge with Acrobat Pro and is available for purchase as a standalone application. Currently, Adobe Designer is available only for Windows.

KEY TERM

Form elements—This refers to all the objects on a form that allow user input, such as text boxes, radio buttons, check boxes, dropdown lists, and so on.

There are three ways to create an Acrobat form. First, you can convert an existing form document to PDF and use Acrobat to add interactive **form elements** to it, such as check boxes and pop-up menus. Second, you can simply create a new form from scratch in Designer, or third, you can create a new form using one of Designer's many templates and sample forms.

If you are creating a PDF form based on an existing paper document, you have limited creative options. After all, the content and structure of the form are already set. However, if you are creating a new form, you have a wide variety of design options and interface elements you can use. You decide how the information will be presented, how the participants will respond, and how their responses will be delivered back to you.

47 About PDF Forms

KEY TERM

HTML—This stands for Hypertext Markup Language, a language used to define how text and images are displayed on the Web.

There are several advantages to PDF forms versus paper forms or **HTML**-based forms. PDF forms provide a fast and convenient method for form distribution and information retrieval. Paper forms need to be faxed, which is often inconvenient and always results in poor visual quality, or they must be sent by postal mail, which is also inconvenient and very slow. Another advantage of PDF forms is that changing the content and information within a PDF form is easy. For example, if you need to change a list of possible responses, you can simply go into Acrobat or Designer and change the items in a drop-down list. In a paper document, you have to revise and reprint the original document, possibly requiring major changes to the document's layout.

Unlike HTML forms, which require an image of the text to ensure the integrity of the font style used, all fonts and images can be embedded into a PDF form. With an HTML form, these images need to be saved to a separate folder, causing delays in uploading the form to a web browser and increasing the chances of file structure problems causing the form to be displayed improperly.

Another advantage to creating a PDF form is that the integrity of the form is maintained across different platforms. Font style, size, and layout remain constant, regardless of whether the form is viewed on a computer running Windows or Mac OS or different web browsers, such as Internet Explorer, Netscape, Safari, or Mozilla.

PDF forms also allow digital signature fields. After the form is filled out, the reader can attach her digital signature to show proof that the form was approved or that all the information provided is accurate.

The three types of PDF forms are **interactive forms**, **dynamic forms**, and **static forms**. Interactive forms enable end users to enter data and have it electronically delivered, either by email or to a database. Dynamic forms are interactive forms that adjust to the amount of content being input by the end user, and static forms are the opposite of dynamic forms—they do not adjust to end user input.

48 About Adobe Designer

Adobe Designer is a new application that enables users to create forms from scratch instead of having to convert a document created in another application into a PDF file and then adding form elements to that document. For years, the vast potential of PDF forms has been hamstrung by the lack of a powerful and user-friendly method for creating PDF forms. Although it's too soon to know whether Designer is going to be the key to widespread adoption of PDF forms, it is a wonderful tool and will be a boon to IT and design professionals in any corporate environment.

Designer users can choose from standard, sample, or custom templates, or they can use existing documents as form templates. Designer takes form creation beyond the basics of a simple form. For example, you can include a barcode in your form, so when the user fills it out and returns it to you, all you need is a common barcode scanner to extract the data from the form. Also, for the more advanced form designer, you can include an XML schema to create extremely powerful, interactive forms.

The Designer form tools make every aspect of PDF form creation easier than ever and enables you to do things you simply cannot do with Acrobat alone.

KEY TERMS

Interactive forms—Forms that allow end users to enter data directly into a form and have it electronically delivered either by email or to a database.

Dynamic forms—Interactive forms that adjust to the amount of content to be displayed and how much information is entered by the end user.

Static forms—Forms with a fixed area for data display and input. If the information entered into a static form is more than the space allows for, the information is not captured.

49 About the Designer Workspace

The Adobe Designer Workspace is designed to be an efficient workspace for form creation. The main window in Designer is the **Layout Editor**. The **Layout Editor** displays the current form and contains four tabs:

- **Body Pages**—This is where you create and edit a form's content. Content from the **Master Pages** can be viewed in the **Body Pages** but cannot be selected.

- **Master Pages**—These contain the layout of the form. You create the background form design in this tab. Content from the **Body Pages** is not shown on this tab.

- **XML Source Pages**—These contain the XML source code for the form. Designer automatically adds the new source code as you create your form.

- **PDF Preview**—This is available only if you have Acrobat or Adobe Reader installed on your computer. The **PDF Preview** allows you to preview your form and test it to ensure it is functioning properly.

Palettes assist in form creation by providing easy access to the tools you use frequently and hiding the tools you do not need.

The **Library** palette contains three tabs: **Standard**, **Barcodes**, and **Custom**. The **Standard** tab displays the various fields and objects to place on the form, including **Text Field**, **Text**, **Numeric Field**, **Password Field**, **Check Box**, and **Button**, just to name a few. The **Barcodes** tab displays the most commonly used barcodes. The Custom tab contains predefined objects, such as an Address Block field, Current Date field, and U.S. States drop-down menu, that can be used as-is or modified to best fit your form.

Other available palettes are as follows:

- **Accessibility**—Enables you to add custom text for screen readers and change the default order in which screen readers search for text.

- **Border**—Enables you to change the border properties for an object.

- **Data View**—Displays the fields from a data source in a hierarchical view.

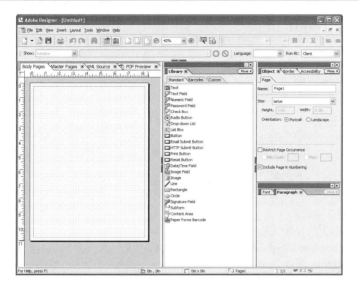

- **Drawing Aids**—Enables you to show the grid, snap to the grid, display a horizontal or vertical ruler, show guidelines, and change the grid and ruler settings.

- **Font**—Enables you to change the font style, size and family of the object.

- **Hierarchy**—Displays a graphical representation of the objects used in a form.

- **How To**—Displays helpful tips for common procedures in Designer.

- **Info**—Displays the metadata associated with the selected objects.

- **Layout**—Displays the dimensions of the selected object, including the anchor point, margins, and the caption position.

- **Library**—Displays all the objects available to use in a form. Objects are divided into three categories: Standard, Barcodes, and Custom.

- **Object**—Enables you to change specific properties of an object, such as field type, appearance, value, and binding.

- **Paragraph**—Enables you to change the alignment, indentation, and spacing of selected text.

- **Report**—Displays information on bindings and warnings of all objects used in the form design.

To display the various palettes, select them from under the **Window** menu. By default, the **Object**, **Layout**, **Border**, and **Accessibility** palettes are grouped together on the right side of the workspace. The **Library** is displayed in the middle of the workspace, and the **Hierarchy** and **Data View** palettes are located on the left side of the workspace.

The **Font** and **Paragraph** palettes appear as a floating box but can be added to the workspace by clicking and dragging their title bars to either side of the **Layout Editor**. The **Drawing Aids**, **Info**, and **Report** palettes also appear as a floating box and can be added to the workspace by pressing and dragging it to either side of the **Layout Editor**.

You can move the palettes to any location within the workspace by clicking the title bar and dragging it to the new location. To close a palette, click the close box located in the upper-right corner of each palette.

50 About Designing Forms

Before creating a form, it is very important to have a design plan. Having a form design sketched out before actually creating the form in either Acrobat or Designer saves you a lot of time and headache. It is far easier to erase and redraw lines on a piece of paper or move placeholder objects around in a layout or illustration program than it is to delete, move, modify, or re-create form elements that might have been painstakingly aligned, grouped, or formatted. Following are some things you should keep in mind when designing a form:

- It is important to determine who your target audience will be so you can design your form accordingly. End users who have a disability, such as vision impairment or reduced mobility, should be able to easily navigate around a form using only the keyboard or screen reader. You can set the tabbing sequence in Adobe Designer so the end user can tab from one field to the next in a logical order, instead of using the mouse.

- Determine the type of information you will be gathering and whether you need to provide information to the end user. Forms should be clear and concise. Try to avoid unnecessary clutter that detracts from the information you are trying to convey or gather from the end user. Group related information together and use consistent elements or organizational structures throughout your form.

- If your form contains images or other graphical objects, sketch a rough draft of how you want the form to look. The actual form design can then be done in a design layout program, such as Adobe InDesign, Microsoft Word, or even the Adobe Designer.

- After you've designed and created your form, test it to make sure all the components are working properly. If you are sending data by email, file server, or the Web, make sure that is working properly.

51 Create a New Form

With Adobe Designer, you have the ability to create a more advanced, more interactive form than ever before. In Acrobat, the only way to create a form is to convert a document into a PDF file and then add the form fields. With Adobe Designer, you can create a form from the ground up, ending up with anything from a simple questionnaire to a full-blown, interactive, multimedia form.

1 Open Adobe Designer

From the **Advanced** menu, select **Forms**, **Create New Form**. A **Create New Form** dialog box appears, informing you that Adobe Designer will open to create the new form and that Acrobat will run in the background. If you do not want to see this message again, select the **Don't Show Again** check box. Click **OK** to continue.

2 Create a Blank Form

Adobe Designer makes form creation easy. The **New Form Assistant** window appears and walks you through the steps for creating a new blank form.

Before You Begin

✔ **47** About PDF Forms

✔ **48** About Adobe Designer

✔ **50** About Designing Forms

See Also

→ **52** Create a Form from a Template

→ **53** Create a Form from Another Document

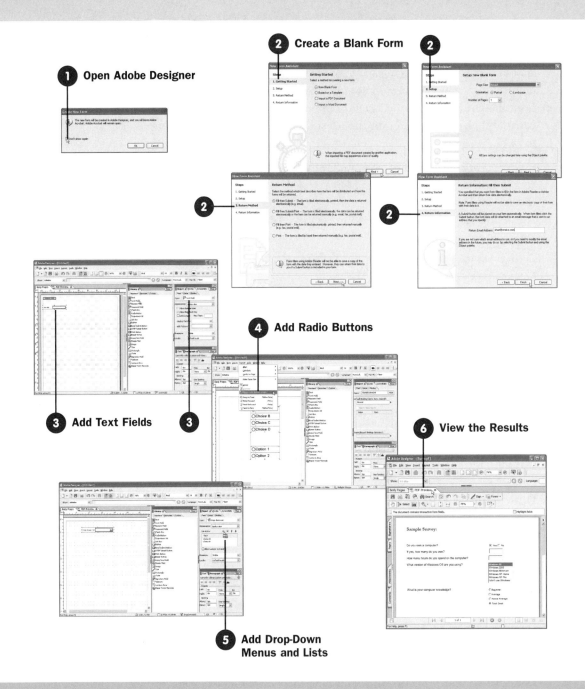

1 Open Adobe Designer

2 Create a Blank Form

2

2

3 Add Text Fields **3**

4 Add Radio Buttons

5 Add Drop-Down Menus and Lists

6 View the Results

Sample Survey:

For **Step 1. Getting Started**, select **New Blank Form**. Choose the page size and layout of your form under **Step 2. Setup**. You can also choose how many pages your form will be from the **Number of Pages** drop-down menu. **Step 3. Return Method** allows you to choose how you want the form data returned to you. You have four choices:

- **Fill Then Submit**—The form is filled out, either through a web browser or Adobe Reader, and the data is then electronically returned, such as through email or a form server.

- **Fill Then Submit/Print**—The form is filled out and can either be returned electronically, such as through email or a form server, or printed and returned manually.

- **Fill Then Print**—The form is filled out electronically and printed, but it is not deliverable by email or the Web.

- **Print**—The end user must print the form first and then manually fill it in by hand. It can then be returned by fax, hand delivery, or postal mail.

Depending on the Return Method you selected, **Step 4. Return Information** displays different options. If you've chosen either the **Fill Then Submit** or **Fill Then Submit/Print** option, you need to enter a return email address. If you have chosen the **Fill Then Print** option, a **Print** button automatically is added to the form. If you have chosen the **Print** option, no further action or information is required. After you have made your selections, click the **Finished** button.

3 Add Text Fields

Now that you have created a blank form, you need to populate it with various containers for information. The most common type of container is a text field, in which the user enters text (alphanumeric) responses. To add a text field to your form, select the **Text Field** object on the **Standard** tab of the **Library** palette. As you move the cursor over the form, notice that it changes into a pencil and text box icon with location coordinates displayed underneath. Click the desired location.

The **Object** tab contains three subtabs:

- **Field**—Shows the type of field currently selected. You can changed the type of field by clicking the drop-down menu and selecting a different field object. You can change the appearance of the text field in the **Field** tab; you can also allow for multiple lines and plain text and limit character length. The **Display Pattern** sets how text entered into the field is displayed, such as a date/time entry, plain text, or a password.

- **Value**—Set the **Value** type of the text field here. If the **Value** type is set to **User Entered—Optional**, users are not required to enter information into the field. If **Users Entered—Recommended** is selected, users do not have to enter information into the field, but a message appears (you need to enter a custom message in the **Empty Message** box). If **User Entered—Required** is chosen for **Value** type, users must enter information into the text field. A custom message, entered in the **Empty Message** box, appears if left blank. The **Validation Pattern** requires that the values entered into the text field match the set pattern. If not, an error message appears. A custom error message can be written in the **Validation Pattern Message** box to replace the standard error message.

- **Binding**—Click this tab and set the name of the text field in the **Name** box. Set the **Default Binding**, which is the type of data-binding method used, to **None**, **Normal**, **Global**, or **New Data Connection**. **Data Pattern** sets the type of data that can be entered in the text field, such as a date/time, plain text, a phone number, a password, or even an email address. The **Data Format** can be set to **Plain Text**, which includes only the value of the UTF-8-encoded text entered, or **XHTML** (Extensible Hypertext Markup Language), which includes the XHTML information for the entered text. **Import/Export Binding** allows a Web Service Definition Language (WSDL) connection.

4 Add Radio Buttons

Radio buttons can be grouped together to form an *exclusive group*, meaning that only one radio button can be selected at a time within that group. This is appropriate for most multiple-choice questions, where the user has to pick one out of a set of responses.

To add a radio button to a form, select the **Radio Button** tool in the **Standard** tab in the **Library** palette. Move the cursor to the desired location for the radio button and click. Repeat this step for each radio button needed. When adding radio buttons to the form, they are automatically grouped together in an exclusive group. If you add a different field, such as a check box or text field and then add another radio button, that new radio button is not included in the previous exclusive group. Instead, a second group is started.

To add a radio button to a previously defined exclusive group, click, drag, and drop the new radio button within the border of the exclusive group. Adjust the alignment if necessary.

To combine two exclusive groups, select the radio buttons in each group by clicking and dragging a box around the two groups. Under the **Layouts** menu, select **Merge Radio Button Groups** to combine them.

To move a radio button from one exclusive group to a different group, select the radio button and drag it within the borders of the other group.

It is important to ensure that the value for each radio button within the group is unique. To change the value of a radio button, select that radio button and click the **Binding** tab in the **Object** palette. Double-click the **Value** associated with that radio button, enter the new value, and either click a different value or press **Enter** to accept the changes.

5 Add Drop-Down Menus and Lists

Drop-down menus and lists provide the user with a selection of responses from which to choose. Drop-down menus show only one selection until the user opens the list. Lists, on the other hand, display more of the choices available to the user.

KEY TERM

Exclusive groups—Groups of radio buttons among which only one button can be active at a time. A common example is a multiple-choice questionnaire. Each question has an exclusive group of responses, among which the user can choose only one.

TIP

Another way of moving a radio button to a different exclusive group is from the **Hierarchy** palette. The **Hierarchy** palette shows the complete structure of a form, including all the exclusive groups of radio buttons. If the **Hierarchy** palette is not visible, you can display it by going to the **Windows** menu and selecting **Hierarchy**. Click and drag the selected radio button to the new exclusive group. Designer automatically changes the name of the radio button to match the others within the group.

TIP

You can also add check boxes to your form. Check boxes are used to indicate a Yes or No value. When the check box is selected, or turned on, the default value is Yes. Otherwise, when not selected, the value for the check box is No. To add a check box to a form, select the **Check Box** tool in the **Standard** tab in the **Library** palette. Click the cursor on the desired location to add the check box. Rename the check box in the **Binding** tab's **Name** box.

TIP

If you prefer not to use the **New Form Assistant** window, you have the option to turn it off. In the lower-left corner of the **New Form Assistant** window is the **Don't Use Assistant** link. When you click this link, the **Assistant Options** window appears. You can select from the following commands: **Skip the Assistant This One Time**, **Skip the Assistant When Creating New Document**, and **Never Show the New Assistant Form Again**. After you have made your selection, click the **OK** button and the **New Form Assistant** window closes.

 TIP

Barcodes are now available in Adobe Designer. You can add barcodes to your form to capture data entered by the user. This data can then be retrieved from a printed return form with a common barcode scanner. Barcode data capture is supported only in Acrobat 7 and Reader 7.

To create a drop-down menu, select the **Drop-Down List** tool on the **Standard** tab. When the cursor has changed to a drop-down box icon to indicate you have selected the **Drop-Down List** tool, click the desired location to add the drop-down list. To add items to the list, under the **Field** tab in the **Library** palette, locate the **List Items** section. Click the plus (+) button and enter the items in the text box provided. Add as many items to your list as necessary. You can change the order of an item by selecting the item and then clicking the **up arrow** or **down arrow**. Assign values to the items under the **Binding** tab by selecting the **Specific Item Values** option. Double-click the value and type in a new value for that item.

Lists are pretty much the same as drop-down menus, except they display all the items available for the user to choose from. Enter items under the **List Items** box in the **Field** tab. To assign values to the items, click the **Binding** tab and select the **Specific Item Values** option. Double-click the value and enter the new value.

6 View the Results

Now that you have created your form, it's time to see how it will look to others and to test it to ensure it is functioning properly.

To view the form, click the **PDF Preview** tab. Designer displays the form as it will look when you save it as a PDF form. Click the various radio buttons and check boxes, select items from the drop-down lists, and enter data into the various text fields. Make any necessary changes and save the form when you are done.

52 Create a Form from a Template

Before You Begin

✔ **47** About PDF Forms

✔ **48** About Adobe Designer

Although it is wonderful that Designer gives you the ability to create a PDF form from scratch, until you have some experience with PDF form creation you might find yourself at a loss as to where to begin. This is where templates come in. In fact, even for experienced form designers, templates can be extremely useful as a starting point for form creation or as an inspiration for generating design ideas. Designer comes with a variety of template types and styles, allowing you to choose the right template based on how the form will be used or how you want it to look.

① Select a Template

② Set Up a Template

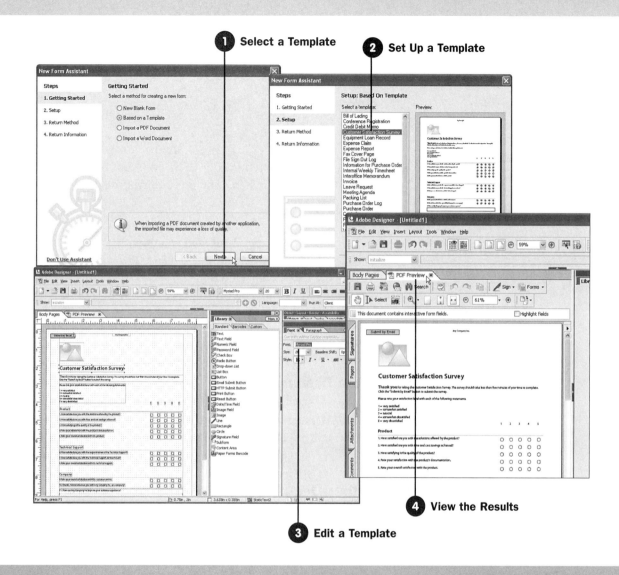

③ Edit a Template

④ View the Results

① Select a Template

With Adobe Designer open, under the **File** menu, select the **New** command. This opens the **New Form Assistant** window. Select **Based on a Template** as your form creation method for **Step 1. Getting Started**. Click the **Next** button to go to step 2.

② Set Up a Template

Select a template in **Step 2. Setup**. In the middle of the **New Form Assistant** window is a list of available form templates. To the right is a graphical preview of what each template looks like. Select the template design you want to use. Click the **Next** button to continue to the next step. After selecting the template design, you need to choose a return method type in **Step 3. Return Method**. Form data can either be returned electronically or by fax/mail. You can enter a return email address in **Step 4. Return Information**.

③ Edit a Template

Now that you have chosen a template, you might choose to use the template as a guideline to create your own PDF form. Or, you can modify the template by adding, deleting, or modifying the fields to create a PDF form that works best for you. To change the properties of a field, select the field and make the necessary changes in the **Object** palette. You can alter how the field looks by making changes in the **Border** and **Font** palettes.

④ View the Results

To see how the PDF form will look to the user, select the **PDF Preview** tab. Designer displays the form as if it were a real PDF file.

53 Create a Form from Another Document

Before You Begin

✔ **①** Create a PDF in Acrobat

✔ **14** Create PDFs from Microsoft Office

If you have an existing document in either MS Word or PDF format, you can use it to create a PDF form. When using a document other than a PDF, Designer automatically converts the document to a PDF, eliminating the need to have to first convert the document in Acrobat.

① Select the Form Creation Method

From the **File** menu, select the **New** command. This opens the **New Form Assistant** window. If you are creating the form from a PDF, select **Import a PDF Document** for **Step 1. Getting Started**. If you are creating the form from a Word document, select **Import a Word Document**. Click **Next** to go to the next step.

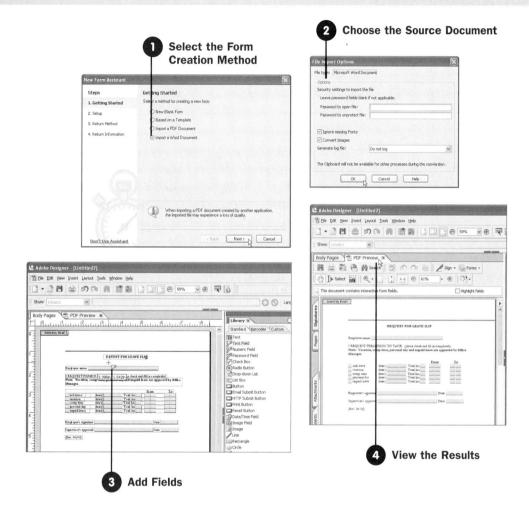

2 Choose the Source Document

1 Select the Form Creation Method

3 Add Fields

4 View the Results

---

2 **Choose the Source Document**

Browse to the location of the source document to complete **Step 2. Setup**. After selecting the document, click **Next** to go to **Step 3. Return Method**. Select how you want the data returned—either submitted electronically by email or sent manually by fax or mail. If you choose to have the data returned electronically, you must enter a return email address in **Step 4. Return Information**. Otherwise, no action is needed for step 4.

When using a Word document, a **File Import Options** dialog box appears after completing the **New Form Assistant**. If the Word document requires a password to open, enter the password in the **Password to Open File** box. If the Word document was protected and only certain areas of the document are editable, remove the protection by typing the password in the **Password to Unprotect File** box.

Designer detects whether the font used in the Word document is available on your computer. If it is not, you can choose to install the font; otherwise, select the **Ignore Missing Fonts** option and Designer substitutes the unknown font with an available font. If you do not select the **Ignore Missing Fonts** option, an Adobe Designer error message appears, informing you that the font is missing and prompting you to either install the font or check the **Ignore Missing Fonts** option.

You can also choose to have Designer convert and embed images when importing the Word document. If you leave the **Convert Images** option unchecked, Designer inserts placeholders for the images.

Designer gives you the option to generate log files. These files contain information about the converted file, such as the filename and conversion process. If you choose not to create a log file, select **Do Not Log**. Otherwise, choose the location to save the log from the drop-down menu.

3 Add Fields

After the form has been selected or converted from another document, you can add fields. From the **Standard** tab in the **Library** palette, select an object tool, such as **Text Field**, **Check Box**, **Drop-down List**, or **Button**. Then click the blank form to add the field.

4 View the Results

After adding the various fields to your document, you can preview how it will look to users by clicking the **PDF Preview** tab. Designer displays the form as it will look to the user. At this time, you might also want to test the fields to ensure you have set the properties correctly and that all the information displayed is accurate.

54 Create a Form in Acrobat

For the user who prefers to create a PDF form in Acrobat, Mac OS users, or Acrobat Standard users who do not have Adobe Designer available to them, you can create your form within Adobe Acrobat. You won't have all the options available to you that you would have in Designer, and you won't be able to use the wizards and templates, but you can create robust and professional forms with all the interactive elements that you would want.

Before You Begin

✔ 1 Create a PDF in Acrobat

✔ 4 Create PDFs from Microsoft Office

✔ 47 About PDF Forms

See Also

→ 55 Send Form Data Through the Web

1 Open the Source Document

The main difference between creating a form in Acrobat versus Designer is that in Acrobat you must start with an existing form document. This document must have all the text labels and graphic elements in place already; you use Acrobat to add the actual interactive elements such as text fields, check boxes and radio buttons, pop-up menus, and drop-down lists. For example, you can create the original form document in Adobe InDesign, convert it to a PDF, and then add the interactive form elements to it in Acrobat.

From the **File** menu, select the **Open** command and browse to the file you will be using as the basis for your PDF form. If you are using a document other than a PDF, under the **Create PDF** submenu, select the appropriate command, such as **From File**, **From Scanner**, or **From Multiple Pages**. Acrobat converts the documents into a PDF.

2 Add Text Fields

If not already displayed, from the **Tools** menu, select **Advanced Editing**, **Show Forms Toolbar**. This opens the **Forms Toolbar**. Click the **Text Field** tool to select it, and click and drag the mouse cursor to create the text form. After releasing the cursor, the **Text Field Properties** dialog box appears.

Under the **General** tab, enter the name of your text field in the **Name** text box. You have the option to enter a brief description of the text field in the **Tooltip** text box. You can change the border, fill color, and font of the text field under the **Appearance** tab.

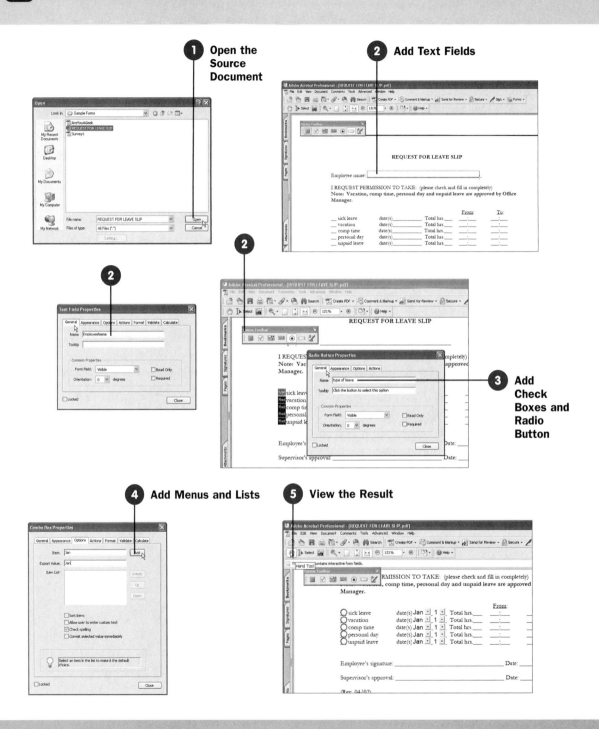

1 Open the Source Document

2 Add Text Fields

2

2

3 Add Check Boxes and Radio Button

4 Add Menus and Lists

5 View the Result

The **Options** tab enables you to set the alignment of the text, whether it's **Left**, **Center**, or **Right** aligned. You can set a **Default Value** of the text box by typing text in the text box provided. Other options available are allowing the text box to be multilined, scrolling long text, allowing rich text formatting, limiting the number of characters in the text box, setting the text as a password so text is displayed as asterisks, having Acrobat check the spelling of the text entered by the user, and finally spacing characters out evenly across the text box by selecting **Comb of Characters** and entering the number of characters.

You can change the format of the text box under the **Format** tab. Categories include the following:

- **Numbers**—Allows you to change the decimal place and type of separator, such as placement of a comma, country currency symbol, and how to display negative numbers

- **Percentage**—Sets the decimal place and separator style

- **Date**—Lets you set how you want the date to be displayed, such as m/d/yy, mm/dd/yy, or mm/dd/yyy

- **Time**—Sets how time is displayed on the form, such as HH:MM or HH:MM:ss, or you can even create your own custom time display by combining the various time formats

- **Special**—Allows for specified text entry, such as ZIP Codes, phone numbers, Social Security numbers, and arbitrary masks

- **Custom**—Lets you create your own custom formatting with JavaScript

You can also restrict the information entered in the text field by the user under the **Validate** tab, such as only allowing alphabetic text in the text field. You can run JavaScript to also validate the information entered into the text field by selecting the **Run Custom Validation Script**, clicking the **Edit** button, and entering the JavaScript in the **Create and Edit JavaScript** window.

Select the **Calculate** tab when working with numbers in the text box. Acrobat can perform simple calculations such as the sum, average, minimum, or maximum of numeric values in a set range of text boxes. For more advanced mathematical calculations, you

NOTE

To view or edit the properties for an existing form
element, select the tool
that was used to create the
object from the Advanced
Editing toolbar. Then
double-click the object or
right-click the object and
select the Properties command. Once in the
Properties dialog box,
make any desired changes.
These changes are immedi-
ately applied to your object.

can enter custom JavaScript in the **Custom Calculation Script** by
clicking the **Edit** button and entering the script in the **Create and
Edit JavaScript** window.

3 Add Check Boxes and Radio Buttons

Check boxes and radio buttons are similar in many ways. Select
either the **Check Box** tool or **Radio Button** tool and click and drag
the cursor at the desired location. When you release the mouse, the
Check Box Properties box or **Radio Button Properties** box
appears.

Under the **General** tab, enter the name in the **Name** field. You can
set the common properties of the form field to be **Visible**, **Hidden**,
Visible but Doesn't Print, or **Hidden but Printable**. If you select
the **Required** option, the user will be required to take action on
this field before saving the form.

The **Appearance** tab lets you change the border and fill color,
along with the font, font size, and color.

The **Options** tab for check boxes allows you to change the check
box style. The check box can be the standard check mark in a box,
or you can choose from one of the following other marks: circle,
cross, diamond, square, or star. The default **Export Value** is **Yes**.
This means that, if the data is exported, the value for this field is
marked as **yes** or **true**, indicating this option was selected on the
form. Select the **Check Box Is Checked by Default** option if you
want the box to be checked by default.

The **Options** tab for radio buttons enables you to change the button style. Such choices include a check mark, circle, cross, diamond, square, and star. By default, the **Export Value** is set to **Yes**.
Select **Button Is Checked by Default** to set the button default to
yes. The important difference between check boxes and radio buttons is that with radio buttons, only one out of a set can selected at
one time. To designate a set of radio buttons, give them all the
same name in the **General** tab. With check boxes, some, none, or
all can be selected in the same set.

4 Add Menus and Lists

To place either a drop-down menu or list, select the **Combo Box**
tool or **List** tool in the **Forms** toolbar. (Drop-down menus are also

referred to as *combo boxes*.) Click and drag the cursor to create the menu box. When you release the cursor, the **Combo Box Properties** dialog box appears. Type a name for the combo box in the **General** tab under **Name**. To add items to the combo box, click the **Options** tab. In the **Items** box, add the items you want to display in your list. You must also enter a value in the **Export Value** box. This value is what is captured when the information provided by the user is gathered either by email or a database. Click the **Add** button and continue to add items. If you need to change the order in which the items are listed, select the item and click the **Up** or **Down** button to move the item accordingly. If you have entered an item in error, select the item and click the **Delete** button to remove it from the list.

Lists are similar to drop-down/combo boxes—the only real difference is that lists display multiple items. Drop-down/combo boxes display only one item until the user opens the menu.

5 View the Result

It is good practice to save your work from time to time. To see how your PDF form will interact, select the **Hand** tool. This takes Acrobat out of the form edit mode and allows you to test your form. Click radio buttons, select items from drop-down/combo boxes, insert text, and see how it is formatted.

55 Send Form Data Through the Web

With Acrobat PDF forms, you can collect data through the Web by either sending it to an online database or a specified email address. To send data to a web server, you need to have a *CGI application* on the server. The Common Gateway Interface (CGI) application collects the data sent from the form and populates a database on that server. Sending data to an email address is much easier because no database setup or CGI application creation is required. You can send either just the data itself or the entire form as an attachment to the email.

1 Select a Form and Create a Button

In Acrobat, open the PDF file you will be using as your form. Insert text fields, check boxes, and other interactive fields as necessary.

Before You Begin

✔ **36** Create a Custom Button

✔ **47** About PDF Forms

✔ **54** Create a Form in Acrobat

🔍 KEY TERM

CGI applications—Small applications that run on web servers. They perform a variety of tasks, including accepting incoming data and storing it in database form.

1 Select a Form and Create a Button

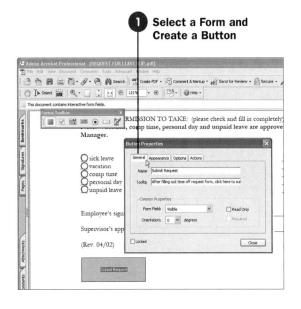

2 Set an Action

From the **Tools** menu, under the **Advanced Editing** submenu, select the **Button** tool. Position your cursor at the desired location and click and drag to create the button. The **Button Properties** dialog box appears. Under the **General** tab, enter the name of your button. You can also set a ToolTip, which is a brief text message of your choice, typically used to describe what the button does when clicked. You can change the appearance of your button, such as border color or borderless, fill color, text size, font color, and font, on the **Appearance** tab.

You can also change the layout of the button on the **Options** tab. You can choose to have text only on your button, an image only, or a combination of both. Behavior selections include **Invert**, which inverts the button; **Push**, which gives the button the illusion of being pressed down when clicked; **Outline**, which outlines the button in a different color when clicked; and **None**, which results in no visible animation of the button when it's clicked.

② Set an Action

To select the action for your form, click the **Actions** tab on the **Button Properties** dialog box. Select **Submit a Form** from the **Select Action** drop-down menu. Click the **Add** button to bring up the **Submit Form Selections** dialog box.

If you are sending the form data to a particular email address, enter **mailto:** followed by the specified email address in the **Enter a URL for This Link** box. For example, enter **mailto:dorian@snako.com**.

If you are sending the form data to a web server, enter the URL address in the **Enter a URL for This Link** box. The CGI script located on the server will know how to interpret the data being sent and populate the database. Make sure the field names match both on the form and the database to ensure the data is properly captured.

10

Reading
Digital Editions

IN THIS CHAPTER:

KEY TERMS

Digital editions—These are books in digital format that can be displayed on a computer or handheld device.

eBook—This is the traditional term for digital editions.

Digital editions, also known as *eBooks*, are electronic books that can be downloaded and read on a computer, a laptop, a dedicated eBook reader, or even a personal digital assistant (PDA). By using Adobe's Portable Document Format (PDF), digital editions have captured the look and feel of a real book by preserving the fonts, graphics, and layout of the actual pages from that book.

Purchasing digital editions has many advantages over buying a traditional book, such as not having to worry whether a book is in stock or having to wait days for it to be delivered. Delivery of a digital edition is immediate. Another advantage to digital editions is portability. Unlike physical books, which can be quite large and cumbersome to transport, you simply download a digital edition to your laptop or PDA and take it with you. Finally, digital editions can be interactive. You can click a link that takes you to the Web for further information or even look up the meaning of unfamiliar words.

56 Activate Your Digital Editions Account

See Also

→ **57** Download a Digital Edition

→ **58** Borrow a Digital Edition

→ **59** View a Digital Edition

Before viewing a digital edition, you must first create and activate your digital editions account. To activate your account, you need to establish an Adobe ID or a .NET Passport account. If you plan on reading digital editions on your PDA, you must install the Adobe Reader for Palm OS, available at www.adobe.com/reader, and reactivate your account on your portable device.

❶ Connect to the Internet

To activate your digital account and download a digital edition, you must have access to the Internet. If you have a broadband connection (DSL or cable modem), you should have a constant connection. If you have a dial-up modem connection, connect to the Internet before proceeding to step 2.

❷ Download a Free Digital Edition

From the **Advanced** menu, under the **Digital Edition** submenu, select the **Adobe Digital Media Store** command. This command opens a browser window that takes you to the **Welcome to the Adobe Digital Media Store** web page. Click the **Preview an eBook** link to download a free digital edition.

1 **Connect to the Internet**

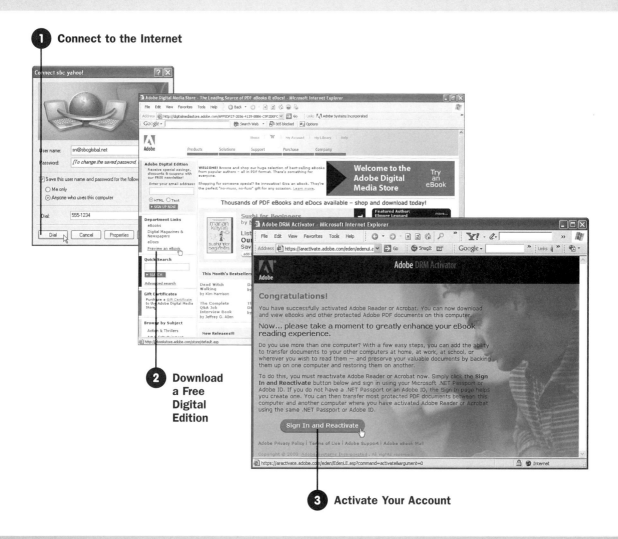

2 Download a Free Digital Edition

3 Activate Your Account

3 **Activate Your Account**

After you have downloaded your free digital edition, a web page opens and prompts you to complete the activation process with either an Adobe ID or a .NET Passport. If you do not have an Adobe ID or a .NET Passport, click the button and follow the instructions to set one up. Then click the **Sign In and Reactivate** button and go through the onscreen prompts to completely activate your account.

57 Download a Digital Edition

Before You Begin

✔ **56** Activate Your Digital Editions Account

See Also

→ **58** Borrow a Digital Edition

→ **59** View a Digital Edition

Now that you have activated your digital editions account, you are ready to start downloading digital editions to your computer, laptop, or PDA. Go to Adobe's digital editions website and browse through the many selections available. You can do a full search for a particular digital edition or browse the various genres, such as mystery, fiction, or poetry. Also available on the Adobe site are links to digital edition/eBook retail sites.

❶ Open My Digital Editions

From the **Advanced** menu, under the **Digital Editions** submenu, select the **My Digital Editions** command. This opens the **My Digital Editions** window. The **My Digital Editions** window shows all the digital editions currently in your library.

❷ Access the Digital Edition Site

While in the **My Digital Editions** window, click the **Adobe Digital Media Store** button. This opens a web browser window to the **Adobe Digital Media Store** web page.

❸ Search for Digital Editions

You can do a quick search by keyword or author's name or, if you have a specific book you are looking for, you can do an advanced search. In an advanced search, you can search by book title, author name, ISBN, language, publisher, subject, or even price. If you would rather just browse the various genres, click one of the selections under the **Browse by Subject** section.

TIP

As your digital editions library grows, you might want to organize the digital editions into categories so they are easier to find. The **My Digital Editions** window contains predefined categories from which you can choose, such as Fiction, History, Mystery, and Romance, plus the option to create or edit a category. Simply select **Edit Categories** from the drop-down menu in the **My Digital Editions** window and either select an existing category to edit or enter a new one in the blank text box.

① **Open My Digital Editions**

② **Access the Digital Edition Site**

③ **Search for Digital Editions**

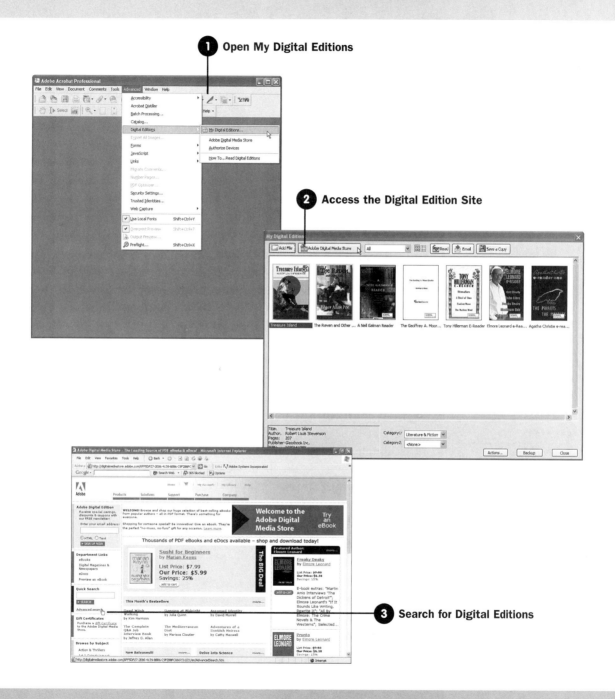

58 Borrow a Digital Edition

Before You Begin

✔ **56** Activate Your Digital Editions Account

See Also

➜ **57** Download a Digital Edition

➜ **59** View a Digital Edition

Just like checking out printed books from a library, you can check out digital editions from online libraries or online bookstores. The advantage to these borrowed digital editions is that you never have to worry about paying late fees again. Digital editions are automatically checked back in for you. Borrowed digital editions are indicated in your **My Digital Editions** window by a thumbnail of the book with a **Time-out** icon next to it.

❶ Borrow a Digital Edition

Adobe has an online digital editions library demo that can be found at the following site: http://librarydemo.adobe.com/library/. Select a digital edition from one of the categories available, such as **Children's Books, Literature & Fiction**, or **Mystery & Thrillers**. Select whether you would like to borrow the digital edition for 1 day or 3 days. Then click the **Add to Bookbag** button. A Bookbag web page appears prompting you to download your eBook. After it is downloaded, a thumbnail of the digital edition appears in your **My Digital Editions** window.

❷ Return a Digital Edition

When you are finished reading the digital edition, you can return it to the library by clicking the **Time-out** icon indicated by a small clock located on the thumbnail of the digital edition. The **Document Expiration** dialog box appears and displays the expiration date, an **OK** button, and a **Return to Lender** button. Click the **Return to Lender** button to return the digital edition. This removes the borrowed digital edition from your **My Digital Editions** window. To close the dialog box, click the **OK** button.

 TIP

To see when a borrowed digital edition expires, click the **Time-out** icon on the thumbnail of the book. When the borrowing period has expired, the digital edition is automatically "returned" and disappears from your **My Digital Editions** window.

 TIP

Some online libraries limit the number of digital editions you can check out at one time, so you might want to get in the habit of promptly returning digital editions so you do not exceed your limit.

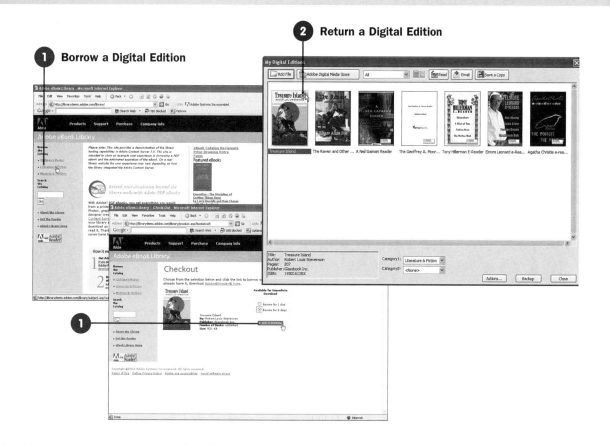

2 Return a Digital Edition

1 Borrow a Digital Edition

---

59 View a Digital Edition

Now that you have selected your digital edition, you can view and read it. When traveling or away from your computer, it's convenient to be able to copy your digital editions to either your laptop or PDA.

1 Open My Digital Editions

From the **Advanced** menu, under the **Digital Editions** submenu, select the **My Digital Editions** command.

Before You Begin

✔ **56** Activate Your Digital Editions Account

✔ **57** Download a Digital Edition

See Also

→ **58** Borrow a Digital Edition

① Open My Digital Editions

② Select a Digital Edition

③ Select an Action

② Select a Digital Edition

Simply click the **Digital Edition** thumbnail to highlight your selection; then click the **Read** button located at the top of the **My Digital Editions** window. If your library is quite extensive, you can select a particular category by clicking the categories drop-down menu; only those books in that particular category are then displayed.

③ Select an Action

Another way to view and read your digital edition is to click the **Actions** button located at the bottom of the **My Digital Editions** window. Other commands available are as follows:

- **Remove**—This action deletes the digital edition from your library.

- **Email**—This command emails your digital edition to a friend.

- **Save a Copy**—This action saves a copy of the digital edition to your hard drive.

- **Check for New Issues**—This command goes out to the Web and checks to see whether any new versions of the digital edition are available to download. If so, it downloads the latest version.

- **Subscription Preferences**—This action brings up the **Subscription Preferences** dialog box, which displays the subscription ID number, when the digital edition will expire, and the option to check for a new issue notification.

- **Visit Subscription Website**—Select a digital edition and then select the **Visit Subscription Website** command. A browser window opens with the website from which you downloaded the digital edition.

- **Send to Mobile Device**—If the publisher has allowed sharing of the digital edition, this action sends a digital edition to your PDA.

- **Return to Lender**—When you are finished reading a borrowed digital editions, simply select it and then select the **Return to Lender** command. The digital edition is then returned.

 TIP

Some publishers of digital editions allow you to turn on the **Read Out Loud** feature and have the digital edition read out loud to you. From the **View** menu, under the **Read Out Loud** submenu, select either **Read This Page Only** or **Read to End of Document**.

 TIP

You can annotate digital editions with comments, highlight selected text, or copy text and objects in Acrobat. If you find a particular passage within the digital edition, you can also use a bookmark to mark its location.

 TIP

One nice feature of digital editions is that they automatically revert to the last open page when you reopen them. This makes it easier to read long files, such as books and magazines, across multiple sessions.

11

Accessibility
for the Disabled

IN THIS CHAPTER:

KEY TERM

Accessibility—When used to refer to PDF files, it means document accessibility for vision- or motion-impaired users.

TIP

With Acrobat 7's new wizard system, setting up a PDF to be accessible is a breeze. From the **Advanced** menu, select **Accessibility, Setup Assistant**. Acrobat walks you step-by-step through the process of creating an accessible document.

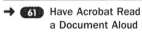

NOTE

Acrobat 7 now allows you to save a PDF and print it to a Braille printer. Under **File**, select the **Save As** command. From the **Save As Type** drop-down menu, select **Text (Accessible)**; then click the **OK** button. Acrobat saves the PDF in a format using a Braille translation application.

With version 7, Adobe Acrobat has gone a step further in making PDF documents accessible to those with vision and mobility impairments. Adobe has created two ways of addressing *accessibility*. The first way is by enabling the author of a PDF to create an accessible PDF or to change an existing PDF to make it accessible. The second way of addressing accessibility is to make navigation and PDF viewing easier for those with disabilities. By changing the view preferences, scrolling options, and **Read Out Loud** command, authors can make their PDFs more accommodating and in line with government standards.

60 Create an Accessible PDF

See Also

→ **61** Have Acrobat Read a Document Aloud

→ **63** Set Automatic Scrolling

Adobe has partnered with screen reader companies to ensure that Acrobat PDF files take full advantage of the latest screen readers and assisted viewing technologies. This is to ensure that users with vision impairments are able to access the information in PDF files as easily as possible. Creating an accessible PDF enables users to make their information accessible to people with a variety of disabilities, multiple platforms, and languages. Any document you create can be changed into an accessible PDF using the Full Check feature, and you can fix any documents that might present accessibility problems.

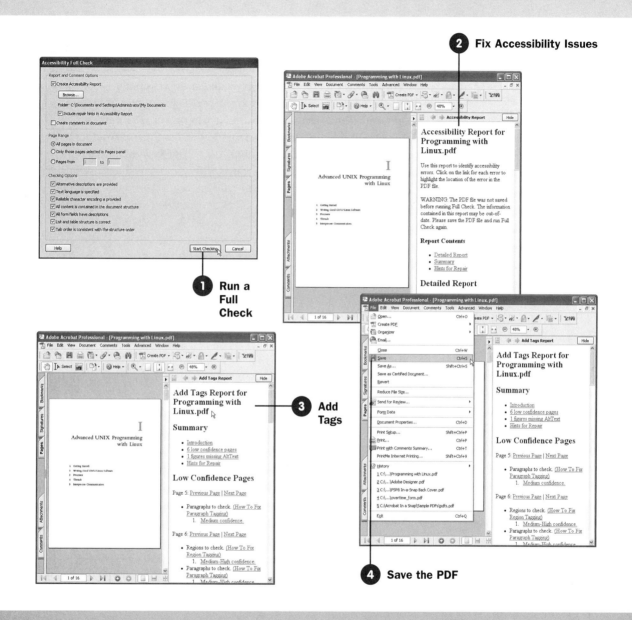

2 Fix Accessibility Issues

1 Run a Full Check

3 Add Tags

4 Save the PDF

1 Run a Full Check

From the **Advanced** menu, select **Accessibility**, **Full Check**.
Although you can also run a quick check, by running a full check
you'll be sure to address all the accessibility options you want.

The **Accessibility Full Check** dialog box has a variety of options to set for checking your PDF. Set the **Report and Comment Options**, **Page Range**, and **Checking Options**. The **Report and Comment Options** area lets you create and save an accessibility report. You can also have hints included in the report to tell you how to fix your PDF document. **Page Range** is where you set whether to check all the pages, the pages selected in the **Pages** panel, or a specific page range. **Checking Options** is where you check or uncheck whether you are provided with alternative descriptions, text language is specified, character encoding is provided, content is structured, described form fields are included, and the list and table structure is correct. The **Tab Order Is Consistent with the Structure Order** check box is used in accessibility mode. It ensures that the user is able to tab through the document objects in the correct *tab order*.

After you have the options set, click the **Start Checking** button; Acrobat runs the full check on the document in the areas specified.

The error dialog box appears, informing you of potential problems with your PDF accessibility.

❷ Fix Accessibility Issues

The **Accessibility Report** pane appears after running a full check on the PDF. In that pane, you can read the **Detailed Report**, **Summary**, and the **Hints for Repair** sections. **Hints for Repair** is particularly useful because it takes you step-by-step through the process of fixing each specific problem.

❸ Add Tags

If your document has never been tagged for *structure*, it must be tagged to be accessible. From the **Advanced** menu, select the **Accessibility**, **Add Tags to Document**. After the tagging has been complete, a **Confidence Log Report** pane appears on the right side of the Acrobat window. This report lists any problems and how to fix them.

❹ Save the PDF

After the document is tagged and a full check run, you must save the file for it to retain the tags. From the **File** menu, select **Save** (to replace the existing file) or **Save As** (to give the file a different name).

61 Have Acrobat Read a Document Aloud

One of the many wonderful accessibility features of Acrobat is the ability to have your documents read to you. The **Read Out Loud** command reads the selected page or the entire document, depending on which option you choose. The voices used are the ones on your operating system. You can get a variety of voices depending on your operating system vendor. For example, the Macintosh OS has a variety of voices to choose from as a standard. The Windows operating system has a more limited range of voices from which to choose.

If the PDF you are having read is tagged, the **Read Out Loud** command reads the document in the tagged structured reading order. If the file is not tagged, the page or document is read from top to bottom and left to right.

1 Read a Document Out Loud

From the **View** menu, select **Read Out Loud, Read This Page Only**. This reads the entire page rather than the whole document. Because all we want to do at this point is get a feel for how the document sounds when read aloud, one page is more than adequate. To stop the reading before the page ends, select the **Stop** command (also located in the **Read Out Loud** submenu of the **View** menu) or press **Ctrl+Shift+E** (Windows) or ⌘**+Shift+E** (Mac OS). To pause the reading, select the **Pause** command (again, located in the **Read Out Loud** submenu of the **View** menu) or press **Ctrl+Shift+C** (Windows) or ⌘**+Shift+C** (Mac OS).

2 Choose a Different Voice

Macintosh users are given a wide variety of voices from which to choose. To pick a different voice from the default one, select the **Reading** tab from the **Preferences** dialog box. The **Preferences** command is listed in the **Edit** (Windows) or **Acrobat** (Mac OS) menu.

In the **Reading** tab, uncheck **Use Default Voice**. Then select a different voice from the **Voice** pop-up menu. To hear each one, you must select it in the **Reading** preferences first and then select the **Read This Page Only** command from the **Read Out Loud** submenu of the **View** menu. An ideal way to hear the various voices is to use the **Pause** command to pause the reading, select another voice, and then continue the reading.

Before You Begin

✔ **60** Create an Accessible PDF

See Also

→ **63** Set Automatic Scrolling

 TIP

Some of the voices you can access are rather funny, but be sure to pick a voice that is easily understood. The whole point of having Acrobat read a document aloud is to make it easier for people with visual impairments to access the information in your document.

① **Read a Document Out Loud**

② **Choose a Different Voice**

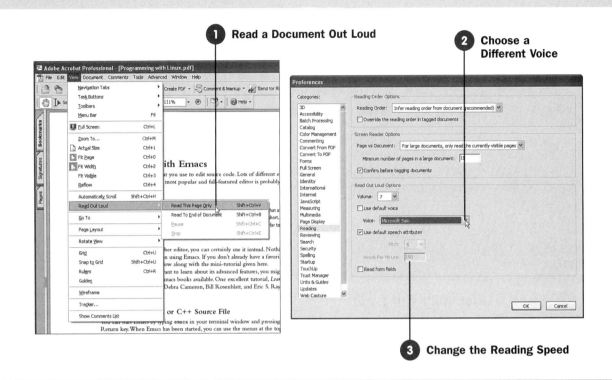

③ **Change the Reading Speed**

③ Change the Reading Speed

Now that you have heard the default voice and other voices, you might want to slow down or speed up the reading speed by increasing or decreasing the reading words per minute. Select the **Reading** tab from the **Preferences** dialog box to change the speed and pitch. Uncheck **Use Default Speech Attributes**. Select a different **Pitch** (a higher or lower voice) from the pop-up menu (a higher number means a higher-pitched voice). Change the **Words per Minute** to a lower number for slower reading or a higher number for faster reading.

62 Change Display Settings for Increased Legibility

Changing Acrobat's display settings can dramatically increase the accessibility of all PDF documents, especially for those with vision disabilities. Something simple like making the page zoom display larger makes all PDF documents easier to read. Along with changing the view, you can set the **Preferred Text Size** setting to be larger.

The default page layout is **Automatic**. If the viewer prefers viewing documents as he does books, simply change the **Page Layout** preferences. These little tweaks to your PDF make a big difference to those with disabilities.

Note that changing Acrobat preferences changes how Acrobat displays all documents, unless the document creator has set specific **Initial View** settings. This task is designed for someone who wants to change his default settings for all documents. For details on how to change the initial view settings for just one document, see **1** **Create a PDF in Acrobat**.

1 Set Zoom Page Display

The **Preferences** command is found under the **Edit** menu (Windows) or the **Acrobat** menu (Mac OS). In the **Preferences** dialog box, select **Page Display** from the list on the left. This determines how your document pages are displayed when opened in Acrobat. Under the **Magnification** section, change the **Default Zoom** pop-up to a larger magnification, such as 200%. After you click **OK**, the next file you open in Acrobat appears at 200% rather than the default of **Fit Page**. Some of your choices, other than a percentage, are **Fit Visible**, **Fit Width**, and **Actual Size**.

2 Check Page Layout

The default page layout is a single page. You might want to change the layout to match how it looks when reading a book by choosing facing pages. Other page layout choices are **Continuous**, **Continuous-Facing**, **Facing**, and **Single Page**. Depending on your audience, select an appropriate page layout.

Before You Begin

✔ **60** Create an Accessible PDF

See Also

→ **63** Set Automatic Scrolling

TIP

Changing the initial magnification and page layout of an individual PDF document (using the **Document Properties** command in the **File** menu) can dramatically increase the accessibility of a document you have created, especially for those with visual impairments. Something simple like making the initial page zoom display larger makes the information displayed much easier to read. Of course, increasing the magnification means that a smaller portion of the document is displayed, which requires more scrolling. You have to judge where the balance lies between making the document easier to read versus requiring more scrolling. One benefits those with visual impairments, whereas the other benefits those with motion impairments.

2 Check Page Layout

3 Alter Page Display Options

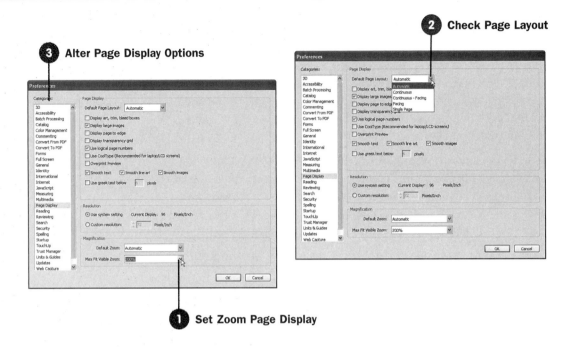

1 Set Zoom Page Display

TIP

Change the zoom size for kids as well. That way, the larger print is easier for beginning readers to see.

3 Alter Page Display Options

Under the **Page Display** area are a variety of check boxes for setting options for the display of the PDF page. If you are sending the file to a printer, check the **Display Art, Trim, Bleed Boxes** for printer approval. If you have a laptop or LCD screen, check the **Use CoolType** box so the text is more legible. When using transparency in the PDF, check the **Display Transparency Grid** so the viewer understands that the page is transparent.

There are various other options to select from. If you're using large images, you can choose to not have them shown to save time when opening a file. Another item you can set is the resolution. If your file is going to be viewed only on a computer screen, set the resolution to 72 (screen or monitor resolution).

63 Set Automatic Scrolling

You can move around a document in a variety of ways. One way is using the page navigation buttons at the bottom of the Acrobat screen. Another is using your keyboard to go to the next or previous page. You can also set Acrobat to automatically scroll so you don't have to keep clicking to move down a page while you're reading. Find what feels comfortable for you.

Before You Begin

✔ **61** Have Acrobat Read a Document Aloud

See Also

→ **62** Change Display Settings for Increased Legibility

1 Set Scrolling

Under the **View** menu, select **Automatically Scroll**. This starts the document automatically scrolling, gradually moving the page up off the screen and bringing the next page in from the bottom of the screen. As the document is scrolling, you can press any number from 0 to 9 to increase or decrease the scrolling speed (lower numbers are slower speeds, with 0 being no scrolling at all). To stop automatic scrolling, select **Automatically Scroll** from the **View** menu again to uncheck the action.

2 Change Scrolling Direction

While using automatic scrolling, you can easily change the direction in which the document is scrolling. Use the **minus** key on the numeric keypad or the **hyphen** key to change the direction in which the document is scrolling.

3 Jump to the Next Page

When automatic scrolling is on and you want to go to the next page, press the **right arrow** key on your keyboard. To go to the previous page, press the **left arrow** key.

 TIP

To stop scrolling either press the **Ctrl+Shift+H** (Windows) or ⌘**+Shift+H** (Mac OS) keyboard shortcut or simply press the **Esc** key on your keyboard.

1 Set Scrolling

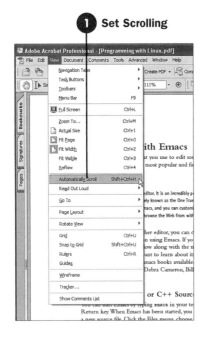

2 Change Scrolling Direction

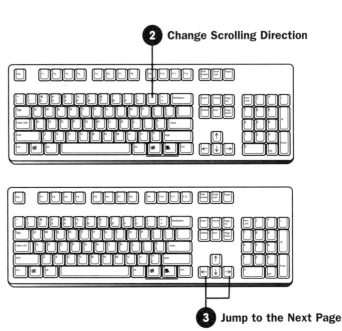

3 Jump to the Next Page

12

Preparing to Print

IN THIS CHAPTER:

With very few exceptions, PDF documents are created with one of three final types of output in mind: They are viewed on the web, printed to a laser printer or other standard business printer, or sent out to a commer-cial print shop for professional printing. In the first two cases, you gener-ally don't have to check for potential problems or alter any settings. Due to the time and expense involved in sending files out to be commercially printed, however, it is recommended that you preflight any PDF docu-ments intended for commercial printing. *Preflighting* is the process of checking your document for suitability with a particular printer or out-put process. See **66** **About Preflighting** and **67** **Preflight a PDF** for more information about preflighting.

In addition to preflighting, Acrobat also includes other tools to help ensure that your PDF document prints successfully. These include trap-ping, transparency flattening preview, and the PDF Optimizer, all of which are discussed in this chapter.

64 About Trapping

When a document containing multiple colors is printed, the printing process normally requires several passes, one for each color. If the paper is not perfectly aligned during each pass, colors that should appear touching each other sometimes have gaps between them. This is called *misregistration*. To compensate for this misregistration, printers employ a process called *trapping*, where one object slightly overlaps an object of a different color. This slight overlap ensures that, even if the paper is not perfectly aligned during each pass, no gaps appear between colors.

Trapping can be done in either the application in which you created the source document or Acrobat. Acrobat offers numerous ways to set the trapping, including an **Ink Manager**, the **Advanced Print Setup** dialog box, and the **Document Properties** dialog box. However, trapping is not something that the beginning or intermediate Acrobat user should attempt. To quote from Acrobat's own online help:

> "Trapping is a complex process that depends on the interaction of vari-ous color, ink, and printing factors; the correct settings vary, depending on specific printing conditions. Do not change the default trap settings unless you've consulted with your prepress service provider, and read the trapping topics referred to in the following procedures to make sure that you understand how trapping options work in the context of your specific document and printing conditions."

It is valuable to understand what trapping is and to know that you can set trapping options in Acrobat. Each commercial printer you work with will probably have its own method for trapping that works best for its process and specific printing equipment. Usually, they prefer to do the trapping themselves, or at the very least, they will give you specific instructions on how to set up trapping for your PDF document.

65 Preview Color Output

If you need to preview a PDF document's output, Acrobat provides a convenient way to do so with its **Output Preview** dialog box. This dialog box enables you to proof a document's colors, preview separation, and color warnings using the open document window. You can choose from different simulation profiles and color spaces and see both process and spot color plates as well as the ink coverage per plate.

1 View Color

With the PDF document open, click the **Tools** menu and select **Print Production**, **Output Preview**. This opens the **Output Preview** dialog box. Select **All** or one of the following options from the drop-down **Show** menu: **DeviceCMYK**, **Not DeviceCMYK**, **RGB**, **Gray**, **CalGray**, **Calibrated**, **Device**, **DeviceCMYK and Spot**, **Spot Color**, **Images**, **Solid Color**, or **Smooth Shades**.

2 View Separation Plates

When printing documents that use more than one color ink, a separate plate is used for each different color. These colors combine to form the final printed output.

In the **Output Preview** dialog box, select **Separations** from the **Preview** menu. In the **Separations** section, select the box just to the left of the separation plate names. To deselect a separation plate, click the box again to hide the separation. To view all separation plates, select the **Process Plates** box and all separation plates are visible.

See Also

→ **67** Preflight a PDF
→ **72** About Transparency Flattening Preview

NOTE

Although Acrobat's output preview capabilities are impressive, the onscreen separation preview colors that you see most likely won't match the final printed color separation output unless you have been using a color management system with accurately calibrated ICC profiles and have calibrated your monitor.

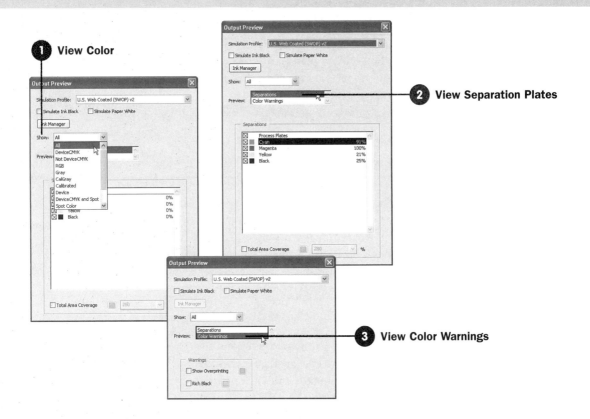

1 View Color

2 View Separation Plates

3 View Color Warnings

NOTE

Depending on the type of paper and the quality of the ink, the color black can often appear with a notice-able brown or purple tint. To get the color black to appear truly black, printers often add other colors to it. Adding some cyan, magen-ta, and yellow ink to black ink creates a deep, dark, and convincing black. This is referred to as *rich black* and is a common practice in the printing industry.

3 View Color Warnings

Viewing a color warning enables you to check whether colors in your document are reproducible on a specified press or if rich black ink will be used instead.

In the **Output Preview** dialog box, select **Color Warnings** from the **Preview** menu. Select **Show Overprinting** in the **Warnings** section to see whether there are any areas of the document where there might be some color bleeding, transparency, or overprinting. You can change the warning color by selecting a different color from the swatch color picker. Select **Rich Black** to see whether any area or text will be printed in rich black. Rich black is black ink mixed with colored ink to give it a richer color and increase opaci-ty, preventing background colors from showing through text or images.

66 About Preflighting

If you plan on having your PDF document printed commercially, you should be sure to preflight it. Preflighting is the process of checking your document against a list of user-defined rules. Preflighting lets you verify that your PDF document contains all the features, fonts, and formatting you want and none that you do not. It analyzes a document to ensure that it is ready to be printed based on predefined settings for various output processes, a settings file you get from your print professional, or custom settings you define.

For example, a preflight profile called **Newspaper Ads** verifies whether a PDF file can be processed as a display ad for a newspaper. Another preflight profile, **Digital Press (B/W)**, verifies whether a PDF file can be processed on a digital press allowing only black and white.

Traditionally, preflighting was something you did to your source document before converting it to PDF and sending it to a commercial printer. With Acrobat 6 Professional, preflighting became a feature of Acrobat, allowing you to preflight documents from a variety of sources consistently and efficiently.

In addition to approximately 50 preset profiles, Acrobat also has the capability to import and export preflight profiles. This allows you to receive a profile from your print professional (via its website, email, or disk), import it into Acrobat, and use it to preflight your document to ensure it will print correctly.

67 Preflight a PDF

Preflighting a PDF is a relatively simple matter. You open the document and select a profile and Acrobat checks your document against the rules contained within the profile. When it is done, it displays a report letting you know which rules, if any, have been violated. This information then allows you to go back to your source document and make any necessary changes.

Before You Begin

✔ **66** About Preflighting

See Also

→ **70** Generate a PDF/X–Compliant Document

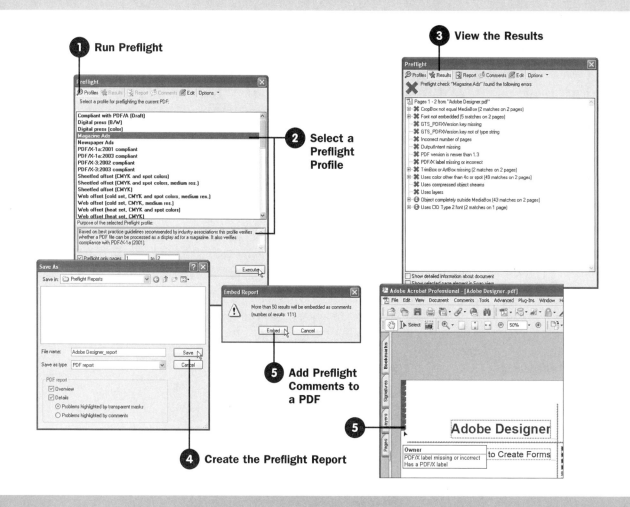

① Run Preflight

③ View the Results

② Select a Preflight Profile

④ Create the Preflight Report

⑤ Add Preflight Comments to a PDF

① Run Preflight

From the **Advanced** menu, select **Preflight**. This opens the **Preflight** dialog box, displaying the **Profiles** window by default.

② Select Preflight Profile

Select a profile from the list box. Notice that when you select a profile, the text box below gives a brief description of that preflight profile. You can apply the preflight profile to a range of pages by selecting the **Preflight Only Pages** option. Click the **Execute** button to run the preflight profile.

③ View the Results

The **Results** window is automatically displayed when Acrobat has finished preflighting. The rules list displays the rules contained in the profile. If a profile rule is violated, a red *X* appears next to that rule.

④ Create the Preflight Report

Click the **Report** command to create a preflight report, which brings up the **Save As** dialog box. The filename is the name of the original file, with _report appended to it. You have a choice of the type of report you want to save it as, such as a PDF, XML, or text report. You also have the option to create an overview and detailed report of the preflight errors of your document. Click the check box next to either or both options.

⑤ Add Preflight Comments to a PDF

Click the **Comments** command to embed the preflight errors into the document as notes. An **Embed Report** information box appears, letting you know how many results will be added. Click the **Embed** button to add comments to the PDF.

68 Edit a Preflight Profile

Acrobat comes with approximately 50 predefined preflight profiles. Any of these can be used as-is or modified. You can also create a new profile with your own custom settings. New profiles appear in the list along with the preset profiles.

① Select a Profile

From the **Advanced** menu, select **Preflight**. This opens the **Preflight** dialog box. Select the profile you want to edit and click the **Edit** button. The **Preflight: Edit Profile** dialog box appears.

② Edit a Profile

Before you edit a profile, it must first be unlocked. Click the arrow on the **Locked** button in the **Preflight: Edit Profile** dialog box, and then select **Unlocked**. After the profile is unlocked, you can modify the rules and conditions. Click the plus sign next to the profile to expand the rules.

Before You Begin

✔ **66** About Preflighting

✔ **67** Preflight a PDF

See Also

➔ **69** Import or Export a Preflight Profile

 TIP

If you would prefer to not alter any of the preset profiles, you can create your own custom profile. To create a new profile, click the **Create a New Preflight Profile** button (the first button under the list of profiles), rename the profile, select a category under the new profile, and set any desired rules. Be sure to click the **Save** button periodically as you are specifying rules.

1 Select a Profile

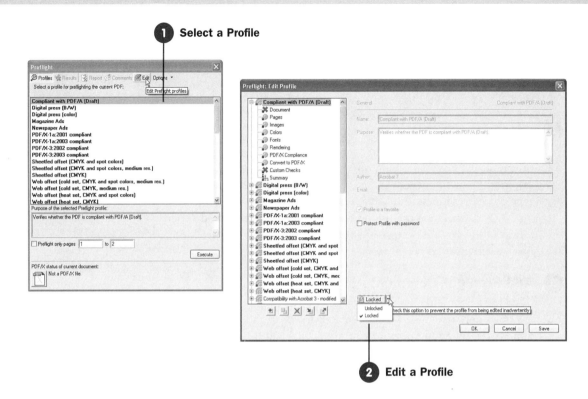

2 Edit a Profile

69 Import or Export a Preflight Profile

Before You Begin

✔ **66** About Preflighting

See Also

→ **68** Edit a Preflight Profile

Preflight profiles can be shared between users by importing or exporting the profile. But before exchanging a profile, it must first be packaged with all the rules and conditions for that particular profile.

1 Select a Profile

From the **Advanced** menu, select **Preflight** to display the **Preflight** dialog box. Click the **Edit** button to display the **Preflight: Edit Profile** dialog box.

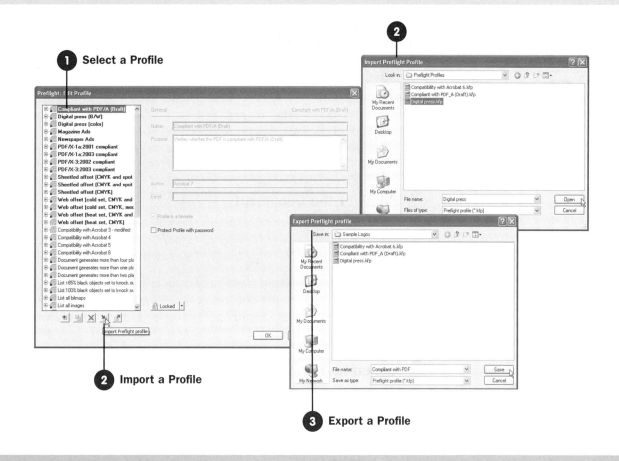

1 Select a Profile

2

2 Import a Profile

3 Export a Profile

2 **Import a Profile**

Click the **Import Preflight Profile** button, browse to the preflight
package file (.kfp extension), and click the **Open** button. The
imported preflight profile now appears in the profiles list.

3 **Export a Profile**

To export a preflight profile, select the profile to export. If you
want to password-protect the profile before exporting, select the
Protect Profile with Password option. Enter the password in the
Preflight: Enter Password dialog box that appears, and click **OK**
to continue. Click the **Export Preflight Profile** button. Browse to
the desired location and click the **Save** button to export the profile.

70 Generate a PDF/X–Compliant Document

Before You Begin

✔ **66** About Preflighting

✔ **67** Preflighting a PDF

PDF/X stands for PDF Exchange and is a subset of the Adobe PDF file format. PDF/X eliminates many of the printing problems caused by color, font, and trapping variables. You can verify whether a document is PDF/X–compliant by preflighting the document within Acrobat. If your document is not PDF/X–compliant, you need to return to the original source document, make any necessary changes, and generate a new PDF.

① Preflight the Document

Open the PDF document in Acrobat. From the **Advanced** menu, select **Preflight**. In the **Preflight** dialog box, select any of the PDF/X–compliant profiles. Click the **Execute** button.

After Acrobat runs the preflight profile on the document, the results are automatically displayed in the **Results** section. Click the plus sign next to each violation to see the specific instance where the rule was violated.

② Generate a Report

Click the **Report** command at the top of the **Preflight** dialog box. A **Save As** dialog box appears. Name the file and specify a location; then click the **Save** button. You can choose to save an overview or detailed version of the report.

③ Correct the Original Source Document

Open the preflight report as well as the original source document. Make any necessary changes to the source document as detailed in the report. Save the source file and generate a new PDF document from it.

④ Repeat Preflight

Return to step 1, open the updated PDF document, and preflight it using the same PDF/X–compliant profile. Repeat this process until the document is PDF/X–compliant.

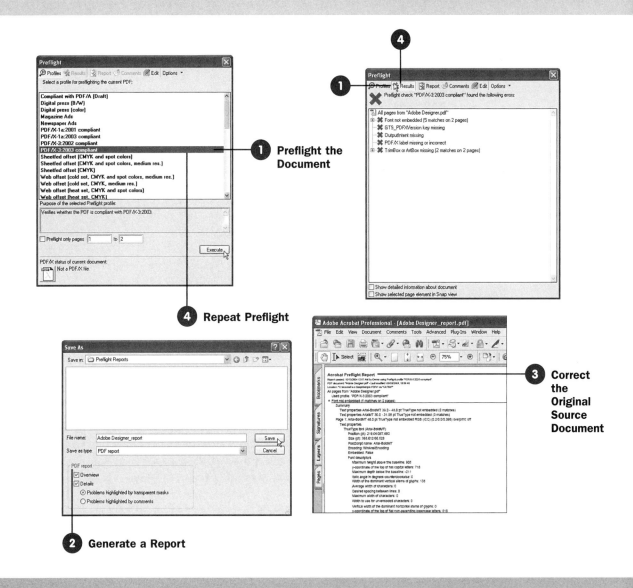

1 Preflight the Document

4 Repeat Preflight

3 Correct the Original Source Document

2 Generate a Report

71 Edit Preflight General Preferences

The **Preflight General Preferences** dialog box lets you change display settings for your preflight reports. You can change how many results are displayed per page for various types of checks, as well as the degree of detail.

See Also

→ **67** Preflight a PDF

1 Display Preferences

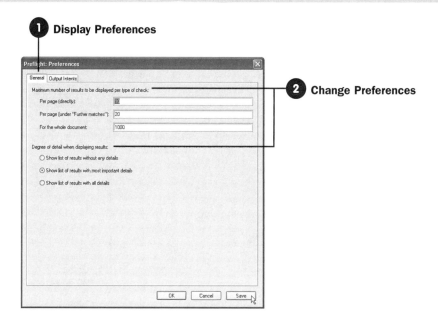

2 Change Preferences

1 Display Preferences

From the **Advanced** menu, select **Preflight** to display the **Preflight** dialog box. When the profiles have finished loading, click the **Options** button and select the **Preflight Preferences** command. The **Preflight: Preferences** dialog box is displayed.

2 Change Preferences

On the **General** tab are two preferences you can change. **Maximum Number of Results to Be Displayed per Type of Check** lets you change how many results you would like to display per page. **Degree of Detail When Displaying Results** lets you choose from three options to show results without any detail, show results for only important details, or show all details. Remember to click the **Save** button to save any changes you have made to the preflight preferences.

72 About Transparency Flattening Preview

Transparency flattening is a process wherein Acrobat cuts apart partially transparent, overlapping objects to form discreet nonoverlapping objects. This flattening occurs whenever you print a document that contains such objects or save it to a format other than Adobe PDF 1.4 or higher (Acrobat 5.0 or later).

To preview transparency flattening, with your PDF document open, select **Tools**, **Print Production**, **Transparency Flattening**. This displays the **Flattener Preview** dialog box. Within the dialog box are three sections: section 1, section 2, and section 3.

Preview Settings allows you to select different highlight types. Not all options are available for all PDF documents. Availability of highlight options is determined by the content of the object or image and the flattening settings predefined under the **Transparency Flattening** panel in the **Advanced Print Setup** dialog box. To access the **Advanced Print Setup** dialog box, from the **File** menu, select **Print**, and then click the **Advanced** button. At any time, you can click the **Refresh** button to refresh the preview of the PDF and any changes you have made to the preview settings.

Select the following options in the **Flattener Settings** section of the **Flattener Preview** dialog box:

- **Raster/Vector Balance**—Drag the slider or enter the degree of rasterization to be applied to the document.

- **Line Art and Text Resolution**—Set the resolution to rasterize all objects in the document, from 72 to 2400 pixels per inch (ppi).

- **Gradient and Mesh Resolution**—Choose a resolution from 72ppi to 2400ppi for gradients and meshes that have been rasterized due to transparency flattening.

- **Convert All Text to Outlines**—Ensures that the width of all artwork text remains consistent, but it can cause small fonts to appear noticeably thicker.

- **Convert All Strokes to Outlines**—Ensures that the widths of all the lines in the artwork remain consistent, but it can cause thin lines to appear noticeably thicker.

KEY TERM

Transparency flattening—A process of analyzing partially transparent, overlapping objects and converting them into individual nonoverlapping objects that have the same appearance as the previously overlapping objects.

TIP

You are not limited to a maximum resolution of 2400ppi in the **Flattener Preview** dialog box. You can enter resolution values of up to 9600ppi by typing them under **Line Art and Text Resolution** and **Gradient and Mesh Resolution**

TIP

You can enlarge the preview of the document by clicking in the preview area. You can reposition the document within the document area by holding down the spacebar while dragging the mouse. After doing either of these actions, you can return to the original settings by clicking the **Refresh** button.

- **Clip Complex Regions**—Reduces artifacts that result when vector and raster artwork overlap.

- **Preserve Overprint**—Blends the color of transparent objects with the background color to create an overprint effect.

- **Apply to PDF**—There are three options to select from when applying transparency flattening to the PDF. Select from **All Pages in a Document**, **Current Page**, or a specific **Page Range**. Click **Apply** when done. When the transparency flattening process is done, it cannot be undone.

73 About PDF Optimizer

 NOTE

Exercise caution when compressing images in documents that will be output to commercial printers because some compression methods can make an image unusable in certain print production work flows. Never save an optimized PDF document over the original, unless you are certain that the document does not contain any problematic image compression. You should always talk to your print professional before optimizing any PDF documents you will be sending them.

PDF Optimizer is a feature that can produce smaller and more efficient PDF documents. Unnecessary fonts are unembedded; images are compressed; and extraneous PDF objects, such as embedded thumbnails, hidden layers, and external cross references, are removed.

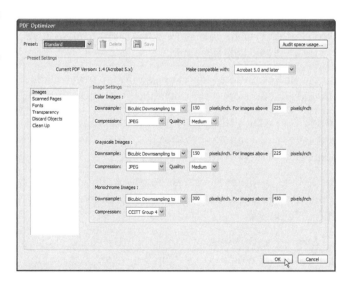

The PDF Optimizer.

From the **Advanced** menu, select the **PDF Optimizer** command to open the **PDF Optimizer** dialog box. The top of the dialog box contains a drop-down list of presets that you can select from, **Delete** and **Save** buttons, and an **Audit Space Usage** button. The **Delete** button is active if you have a custom preset selected and can be used to delete the selected preset. The **Save** button is activated as soon as you make any change to an existing preset. Clicking this button lets you save the current settings as a new preset. The **Audit Space Usage** button produces a report of the bytes used and the percentage of total file size for various document elements, such as bookmarks, fonts, comments, and extended graphics states. This information can lead you to areas where optimization will yield the best results.

The rest of the dialog box consists of a list of six categories and options for each category, as follows:

- **Images**—Contains options for down sampling; compression type; and compression quality for color, grayscale, and monochrome images

- **Scanned Pages**—Lets you balance compression versus image quality as well as apply various graphical filters

- **Fonts**—Lets you unembed specific fonts, such as system fonts or fonts you know the user has installed on her computer

- **Transparency**—Enables you to flatten transparency in the document and set flattening options

- **Discard Objects**—Provides a list of objects to discard from the document

- **Clean Up**—Contains miscellaneous optimization settings

13

Using Paper Capture

IN THIS CHAPTER:

KEY TERM

Paper capture—The process of creating PDF files from scanned documents.

TIP

If you have large volumes of pages to convert to PDF, you might consider purchasing Adobe's Acrobat Capture 3.0 software and a high-volume, sheet-fed scanner. Capture offers more options and more robust document conversion and *OCR* features. It is designed for processing up to tens of thousands of pages and comes in both personal and workgroup versions.

KEY TERM

OCR—Short for Optical Character Recognition, a software technology that recognizes text shapes in scanned documents and converts them to editable text.

You can use Acrobat to convert a scanned image of a document into an editable and searchable PDF file. This process is called *paper capture*. Paper capture is useful when you cannot locate the original digital file that was used to create a document or when you need to create a digital version of a printed document. You can convert your paper documents into PDFs for email distribution, archive them to a CD-ROM, or post them on a shared server for fellow co-workers to view.

74 Set Preferences for Paper Capture

See Also

→ **75** Convert a Scanned Document into Text

→ **76** Find OCR Suspects

Before scanning images or other documents and converting them to a PDF, you need to set up your scanner. Acrobat won't recognize your scanner if you don't have the proper software driver installed, and regardless of whether Acrobat recognizes your scanner, it has to function correctly to create an image for Acrobat to convert. Follow the setup instructions for your scanner and make sure it is working properly before using Acrobat to convert the document to a PDF file.

When your scanner is properly configured, you are ready to set up your scanning preferences in Acrobat.

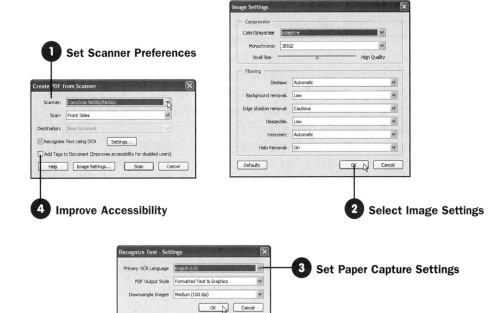

① Set Scanner Preferences

④ Improve Accessibility

② Select Image Settings

③ Set Paper Capture Settings

① Set Scanner Preferences

After you have your scanner set up to scan your documents, from the **File** menu, select **Create PDF**, **From Scanner**. This brings up the **Create PDF from Scanner** dialog box.

From the **Scanner** drop-down list, select your scanner. Then select **Front Sides** or **Both Sides** from the **Scan** drop-down list. From the **Destination** drop-down list, select either **New Document** or **Append to Current Document**.

② Select Image Settings

When scanning an image and converting it to a PDF, you must set up the image settings, which are accessible by clicking the **Image Settings** button in the **Create PDF from Scanner** dialog box. After clicking the **Image Settings** button, the **Image Settings** dialog box, which is divided into two sections, appears.

Under the **Compression** section in the **Image Settings** dialog box, you can change the **Color/Grayscale** option to either **Adaptive** or **JPEG**. Use the **Adaptive** option if your document contains different types of data (text, picture, diagrams, and so on), and use the **JPEG** option for documents that are primarily image-based. You can also change the **Monochrome** option to one of the following: **JBIG2** (slower, high compression), **Adaptive**, or **CCITT Group 4** (faster, less compressed). The compression of the scanned image can be changed by moving the slider bar either to the left, which creates a small file size and lower-quality PDF document, or to the right, which creates a larger file size but a higher-quality scanned PDF.

Several options are found under the **Filtering** section of the **Image Settings** dialog box:

- **Deskew**—Rotates the page so it appears to be vertical and not skewed. You can select **Off** or **Automatic**.

- **Background Removal**—Takes an almost white background and converts it to an all-white background. This can be set to **Off**, **Low**, **Medium**, or **High**.

- **Edge Shadow Removal**—Removes dark streaks at the corners of the pages caused by shadows from the scanner light. You can choose between **Off**, **Cautious**, and **Aggressive**.

- **Despeckle**—Removes black spots from the document. This option can be set to **Off**, **Low**, **Medium**, or **High**.

- **Descreen**—Removes halftone dot structure from scanned images to improve legibility.

- **Halo Removal**—Removes excess color from an object when scanned. You can set this to **On** or **Off** (only on color pages).

Click the **OK** button after making your selections. When you're back at the **Create PDF from Scanner** dialog box, click the **Scan** button to scan your document.

➌ Set Paper Capture Settings

To allow for editing and searchability of your scanned document, select the **Recognize Text Using OCR** option; then click the **Settings** button. This brings up the **Recognize Text - Settings** dialog box.

Acrobat supports 16 languages for Windows and 17 for Mac OS that you can select as the **Primary OCR Language**. Click the drop-down menu to select the appropriate language.

You can choose from two **PDF Output Styles**. The **Searchable Image** option adds text to a hidden layer behind the original image. That text is then searchable, but it cannot be edited. The **Formatted Text & Graphics** option replaces the original font with similar-looking and editable text.

4 **Improve Accessibility**

This is an optional step when converting a scanned image to a readable PDF document. Click the **Add Tags to Document** option if you want Acrobat to add tags for easier accessibility for disabled readers. See **60** **Create an Accessible PDF** for more information on tags and accessibility.

 TIP

If, after you've made changes to the compression and filtering settings, you decide to go back to the original settings, simply click the **Default** button. Acrobat resets the options back to the default compression and filtering settings.

 TIP

When scanning in a document, be sure the words are clear and well formed. If letters are touching or are too thin, adjust the brightness on your scanner: Increase the brightness to separate touching letters, and increase the darkness to make thin letters more legible.

75 Convert a Scanned Document into Text

If you have an existing PDF document that either was scanned without paper capture settings or was created using the **From File** command, you can still do a search and edit of the PDF by using Acrobat's OCR conversion process.

1 **Select the Source Document**

From the **File** menu, select the **Open** command; then browse to the file you want to convert to searchable text and open it.

2 **Start the Capture**

From the **Documents** menu, under the **Recognize Text Using OCR** submenu, select the **Start** command. This launches the **Recognize Text** dialog box. Under the **Pages** section, you have the option to select the entire document to convert to text, the current page, or a specific page range.

Before You Begin

✔ **74** Set Preferences for Paper Capture

See Also

→ **76** Find OCR Suspects

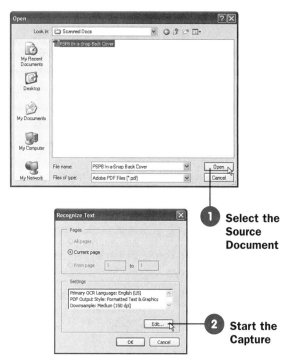

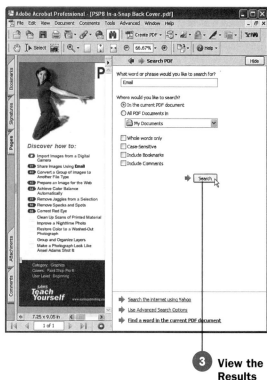

1 Select the Source Document

2 Start the Capture

3 View the Results

Conversion settings are displayed in a text window on the **Recognize Text** dialog box. If you want to change those setting, click the **Edit** button. This opens the **Recognize Text Settings** dialog box. You can then change the **Primary OCR Language**. You can also change the **PDF Output Style** to **Searchable Image (Exact)**, **Searchable Image (Compact)**, or **Formatted Text & Graphics** and change the **Downsample Images** to **Lowest (600 dpi)**, **Low (300 dpi)**, **Medium (150 dpi)**, or **High (72 dpi)**.

Click the **OK** button to start the paper capturing process.

3 View the Results

Acrobat has now converted the PDF into a searchable document. To search for a word or phrase in this document, select the **Search** command from the **Edit** menu. A pane opens on the right side of the document window where you can enter the search text and search options.

76 Find OCR Suspects

Now that you've converted your scanned document into a PDF file that can be searched and edited, you will need to locate any OCR suspects. *OCR suspects* are words or characters that Acrobat might not have interpreted correctly during the paper capture process, therefore Acrobat marks them for review. Not all suspects require changing. For example, acronyms and proper names may be marked as suspect, but in fact, they are spelled correctly. If this is the case, you can leave the word as it is and move on to the next suspect.

1 Find the First OCR Suspect

With your document open, from the **Document** menu, select **Recognize Text Using OCR**, **Find First OCR Suspect**. Acrobat scans through the document and displays the first OCR suspect in the **Find Element** dialog box. If Acrobat displays a character that is not actual text, click the **Not Text** button and Acrobat moves on to the next suspect.

If Acrobat's interpretation of the suspect was correct, click the **Find Next** button. This accepts the word as is and moves on to the next suspect. If the suspect is incorrect, type in the correct spelling of the word in the **Suspect** text box; then click the **Accept and Find** button to accept the new spelling and move on to the next suspect. When you are done, click the **Close** button.

2 Find All OCR Suspects

Another way of finding OCR suspects in your scanned document is to use the **Find All OCR Suspects**. This finds all suspects and displays them in the Acrobat window, with suspects outlined in red.

From the **Document** menu, select **Recognize Text**, **Find All OCR Suspects**. Acrobat then scans the document for all OCR suspects. Click one of the red outlined OCR suspects to bring up the **Find Element** dialog box. Click the **Find Next** button to move on to the next suspect if you do not need to make any changes.

Before You Begin

✔ **74** Set Preferences for Paper Capture

See Also

➜ **75** Convert a Scanned Document into Text

KEY TERM

OCR suspect—Any word or text character that has been flagged by an OCR application as possibly misrecognized. Common culprits are 8s recognized as capital Bs and 0s (zero) or Os (capital 0) recognized as capital Ds.

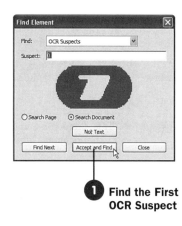

1 Find the First
OCR Suspect

2 Find All OCR Suspects

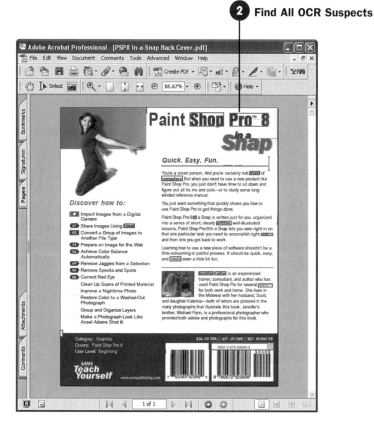

14

Acrobat Distiller

IN THIS CHAPTER:

When you install Adobe Acrobat on your computer, another program, called Acrobat Distiller, is also installed. Most users don't ever launch Distiller or interact with it directly in any way, but it is a vital component in the PDF creation process. This chapter discusses what Distiller is, why it is important, and how and when you might use it.

77 About Acrobat Distiller

See Also

→ **78** About PostScript

→ **79** Change Distiller Settings

Most Acrobat users, when asked the question, "What's the difference between Adobe Acrobat and Adobe Reader?" will say something along the lines of, "Reader only lets you view PDFs. Acrobat creates PDFs." While true in spirit, technically it is the Distiller application that creates the actual PDF file in most cases. Acrobat is used primarily to view, edit, and add functionality to existing PDFs. For this reason, Distiller is often referred to as the "PDF engine" behind Acrobat.

When you print a document to the Adobe PDF printer driver or use the **Create PDF** command from within Acrobat, Distiller converts the document into PDF format, but it does so in the background. You don't see Distiller launch and don't interact with it at all. This is why most Acrobat users are unaware of the role Distiller plays in PDF file creation. If you want to see Distiller for yourself, you can open it directly from the desktop by selecting **Acrobat Distiller 7.0** in the **Programs** submenu of the **Start** menu (Windows) or by clicking the **Acrobat Distiller 7.0** icon in the **Acrobat 7** folder (Mac OS). Within Acrobat, you can launch Distiller by clicking the **Advanced** menu and selecting **Acrobat Distiller**. Incidentally, you can't do anything with Distiller unless you have a PostScript-format file handy. See **78** **About PostScript** for details on the relationship between PostScript, Distiller, and PDF.

The following are three Distiller-related scenarios Acrobat users might find themselves in:

 NOTE

If you need to change Distiller's settings for a single print job, you can do that without launching Distiller. When printing to the Adobe PDF printer, click the **Properties** button in the **Print** dialog box and pick a different setting from the **Default Setting** drop-down list.

- You are creating PDFs from standard business documents for general distribution and printing. The default settings work fine for this, and there is no need to launch Distiller.

- You create large numbers of PDFs for output other than laser printers and want to optimize the output quality (for commercial printing) or minimize the file size (for email distribution or online access) for all print jobs. You need to launch Distiller and choose from one of the predefined settings to change Distiller's default behavior.

- You are preparing a document for commercial printing and have been instructed by your print shop to either change certain settings in Distiller or load a custom settings file from your print shop. You need to launch Distiller and either edit or add settings.

78 About PostScript

Distiller converts documents to the PDF file format, but it can convert only one type of document: PostScript files (including Encapsulated PostScript [EPS] files). It is strictly a PostScript-to-PDF conversion program. Many page-layout and illustration programs allow you to save a file in the PostScript format, but for most users, this is unnecessary. They can simply print directly to the Adobe PDF printer driver, which converts a document into PostScript format and sends it directly to Distiller for conversion into a PDF document.

So, what is *PostScript*? It is a software language, but rather than being a language that tells computers what to do, such as Visual Basic or C++, it tells printers how to print documents. Specifically, PostScript is a *page description language*. With PostScript, every letter, line, and image in your document is precisely and mathematically defined. Any printer that understands PostScript can then reproduce that document. PostScript was invented by Adobe Systems around the same time that the PageMaker page layout application and the Apple LaserWriter were introduced, and together the three of them created the desktop publishing revolution.

PDF is also a page description language, but it is a much more efficient one. It produces smaller files and prints faster than raw PostScript. (PDF files still send PostScript information to the printer, but because the data in a PDF document is better organized, the final output to a printer tends to be faster.) For this reason, most commercial printers prefer working with PDF files. Because PDF also offers the advantages of easy viewing on virtually any operating system and in any Web browser, it's easy to understand why PDF is enjoying ever-growing popularity.

Most popular illustration or page layout applications can output files in the PostScript format because that has traditionally been the format for high-end, commercial printing. Many (including Adobe InDesign and Adobe Illustrator) can create PDF output directly, either by saving as PDF or with an **Export to PDF** command. And, of course, all applications can create PDF output by simply printing to the Adobe PDF virtual printer.

Before You Begin

✔ **77** About Acrobat Distiller

See Also

→ **80** Create Custom Settings

KEY TERMS

PostScript—A page description language that enables printers to output text and images exactly as they appear onscreen.

Page description language—A software language that describes the text and images on a page mathematically for precise reproduction on a printer or other output device.

Where Distiller comes in is in its capability to convert PostScript and Encapsulated PostScript (EPS) files to PDF quickly and easily while offering a high level of control over the process. The three ways to convert PostScript files to PDF with Distiller are

- **Open the file with Distiller**—The **Open** command in the **File** menu lets you locate and open a specific PostScript or EPS file. The file is automatically converted to PDF as soon as it is opened.

- **Drag the file into the Distiller window**—Simply dragging one or more file icons from a desktop folder into the Distiller window converts them all to PDF.

- **Set up a watched folder**—Use the **Watched Folders** command in the Distiller **Settings** menu to set up one or more watched folders. While Distiller is running, any PostScript or EPS files placed in these folders are automatically converted to PDF.

All three of these methods work only with PostScript or EPS files. To convert other file types to PDF, you have to work from within the source application, either by saving/exporting to PDF or by printing to the Adobe PDF virtual printer.

79 Change Distiller Settings

Before You Begin

✔ About Acrobat Distiller

See Also

→ **4** Create PDFs from Microsoft Office

Job options—The term used in previous versions of Distiller for default settings. These settings files still use the `.joboptions` suffix.

For standard business documents, the standard Distiller settings work just fine. For other types of documents, you can get smaller file sizes, faster printing, or better quality by choosing different default conversion settings for Distiller. Once selected, all PDF documents you create will use this new setting until you choose a different setting, so be sure to change back to the standard setting if you work primarily with regular business documents.

1 Open Distiller

From the **Advanced** menu in Acrobat, select **Acrobat Distiller**. The Distiller application launches in a window smaller than many Acrobat dialog boxes. The Distiller application window is divided into four sections:

Adobe PDF Settings contains a drop-down list of installed settings files, traditionally called Distiller *job options*. Helpful text descriptions explain each of the settings in the list.

1 Open Distiller

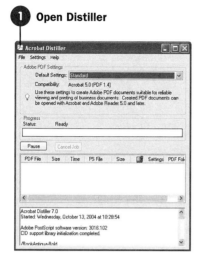

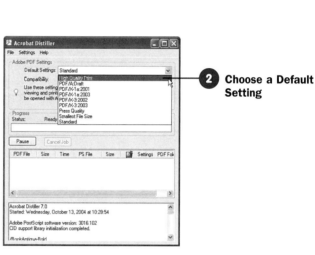

2 Choose a Default Setting

Progress shows a progress bar to let you know how far along the PostScript-to-PDF conversion process is for the current file. The **Pause** and **Cancel Job** buttons let you pause or cancel a conversion in progress.

The file list shows information for each file converted since launching Distiller, including the name and size of the original PostScript or EPS file, the conversion time, and the settings used. You can resize each column of information for easier viewing.

Finally, the text field at the bottom of the window shows information about the most recent conversion, including error messages if a problem was encountered.

2 **Choose a Default Setting**

From the **Default Settings** drop-down list, select the setting that is most appropriate for the type of document you want to convert to PDF. The preset default settings include

High Quality Print for the best results on desktop printers

PDF/A for long-term archival documents

PDF/X for more reliable printing and exchange of graphic content

Press Quality for the best results on commercial presses

Smallest File Size for fast email transfer and online display

Standard for most business documents

Close Distiller when you are done.

80 Create Custom Settings

Before You Begin

✔ **78** About PostScript

Distiller processes PostScript files based on a large number of variables. Changing any of these variables changes the conversion process, resulting in a slightly different PDF file. Some changes produce noticeable and easily understood effects. For example, changing the image compression settings can make the file size smaller or larger, while degrading or improving the appearance of the image. Other changes can seem arcane and have no apparent effect, except in very special circumstances. For example, turning off the **Preserve Level 2 Copypage Semantics** option produces no noticeable difference in the file whatsoever, but it can prevent the file from printing to older image setters. Do not edit Distiller settings without good reason. For most users, the only reason to edit settings will be on the advice of a print professional or technical support person.

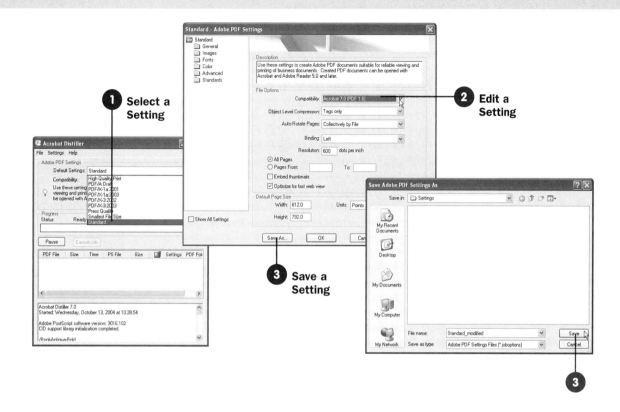

Select a Setting

Choose a setting from the **Default Settings** drop-down list to use as the basis for your new, custom setting. Don't worry about possibly ruining any of these settings. You cannot save your changes over any of these preset settings.

Edit a Setting

From the **Settings** menu, select the **Edit Adobe PDF Settings** command. This brings up the **Adobe PDF Settings** dialog box. The left side of the dialog box shows the current setting and the six settings categories. The rest of the dialog box is made up of the individual settings for the current category.

Go through each category, changing individual settings as desired.

In the **General** category you can enter a description for your new custom setting as well as file and page options such as compatibility, compression, and resolution.

In the **Images** category you can set the downsampling, compression, and image quality for color, grayscale, and monochrome images.

Use the **Fonts** category to set font embedding options as well as to select specific fonts to be always embedded or excluded from embedding.

The **Color** category lets you choose the color settings, management policies, and working spaces for onscreen display and printed output.

The **Advanced** category contains miscellaneous advanced and document structure options.

Finally, the **Standards** category contains options for ensuring that your document is compliant with different subsets of the PDF file format, including PDF/A and PDF/X.

❸ Save a Setting

When you are done, click the **Save As** button. Name your new settings file and click the **Save** button. Do not change the file type or location because Distiller will not be able to use your new custom settings file if you do.

15

Third-Party Plug-Ins

IN THIS CHAPTER:

KEY TERM

Plug-ins—Small software programs that extend the capabilities and functionality of a host application.

TIPS

Because plug-ins are regular files located in an easily accessible folder on your hard drive, you can selectively add or remove individual plug-ins from the plug_ins folder. Simply create a new folder in the Acrobat folder and move unwanted plug-ins out of the plug_ins folder and into this storage folder. You can take this a step further and create custom plug-in sets by creating folders for different circumstances (such as Multimedia, Minimum Memory, or Commercial Printing) and copying the plug-ins you want to use only in those circumstances into the appropriate folder. You can then move your main plug-in set into a storage folder and move all the plug-ins from one of your custom sets into the plug_ins folder while doing a specific type of work. When you are done, you can move the custom set back to its own folder and return your main set to the plug_ins folder for everyday work.

You can disable the loading of all plug-ins by holding down the **Shift** key immediately after launching Acrobat. This is especially useful if you have a plug-in that is malfunctioning so badly (either due to a bug or a conflict with another plug-in) that it is preventing you from using Acrobat at all.

Plug-ins are small software programs that extend the capabilities and functionality of an application. Adobe has been a proponent of plug-ins for a long time and sparked the growth of many small software development companies with its plug-in architecture for Photoshop and Illustrator and its strong support of plug-in developers. This tradition is continued with InDesign and Acrobat. Although most people don't think of plug-ins when they think of Acrobat, many of Acrobat's built-in features are actually plug-ins. Commenting on a PDF, using paper capture, making a PDF accessible and creating web links on a PDF are all examples of Adobe's own Acrobat plug-ins.

81 About How Plug-Ins Work

Before purchasing, installing, and using Acrobat plug-ins, it is helpful to have an understanding of how plug-ins work. This will help you in managing your plug-ins and troubleshooting any problems you might have while using your plug-ins. As mentioned earlier, plug-ins are small software programs that extend the capabilities of a host application, such as Acrobat. When you launch Acrobat, it looks for a folder called plug_ins in the main Acrobat folder and loads into memory any plug-ins it finds there. After these plug-ins are loaded into memory, their functionality is available to you through Acrobat. Most plug-ins offer some sort of interface, usually as a dialog box accessed from the **Plug-Ins** menu. Some plug-ins, however, operate in the background, enhancing Acrobat's functionality without requiring direct user input.

A lot of plug-ins are available, and it's fun to have a lot of added functionality, but the price you pay for all those added goodies is that Acrobat takes up a lot more memory and it takes longer to load the plug-in data from your hard drive. This usually isn't a problem (unless you have a lot of extra plug-ins), but it's important to keep in mind.

82 Install Plug-Ins

Unlike most software, the vast majority of Acrobat plug-ins are purchased via the Internet. Therefore, the process of installing a plug-in requires you to first locate, purchase, download, and extract plug-in software. If you are familiar with downloading and extracting software, you have a head start when it comes to installing Acrobat plug-ins.

1 Select a Plug-In

Navigate to a website and select the desired plug-in. Then select the appropriate operating system. If you are purchasing the plug-in, go through the online purchasing process. If you are downloading a free temporary trial plug-in, follow the instructions for accessing the trial plug-in.

2 Install a Plug-In

After you have saved the plug-in file to a folder on your hard drive, navigate to the folder that contains the plug-in file to install and select the file. Most plug-in files are compressed to a smaller file size for easier storage and faster file transfer. For Windows users, these files usually have a .zip extension. For Mac OS users, the most common file extension is .sit. Double-click the compressed files and follow the onscreen prompts to confirm extraction and select a destination. After the files have been extracted, locate and double-click the extracted file to start the installation of the plug-in. Follow the onscreen prompts to install the new plug-in.

3 View the Results

After you have downloaded, extracted, and installed the plug-in, it is loaded into memory the next time you launch Acrobat. Before using the plug-in for the first time, though, you might need to configure it. Usually, this means setting the preferences for the plug-in.

To set preferences for a plug-in, select the plug-in located under the **Plug-Ins** menu. The **Plug-Ins** menu lists all third-party Acrobat plug-ins installed on your hard drive. Depending on the plug-in, it might not always be available to use unless you have a document open in the active window.

Before You Begin

✔ **81** About How Plug-Ins Work

See Also

→ **83** About Sources for Plug-Ins

💡 TIP

There are two different categories of plug-ins: certified and non-certified. Certified plug-ins are created by Adobe Systems and meet certain standards set by Adobe. Plug-ins from third party developers do not necessarily meet these same standards and so are non-certified plug-ins. By default, Acrobat will load both types of plug-ins. If you experience problems with Acrobat that you suspect might be due to third-party plug-ins, you can tell Acrobat to load only certified plug-ins. To do so, go to the **Edit** menu and select **Preferences**. In the **Preferences** dialog box, select **Startup** in the **Categories** list. In the **Application Startup** section, check the **Use only certified plug-ins** option. The **Currently in Certified Mode:** field displays **Yes** if only certified plug-ins are loaded into memory or **No** if you have certified and non-certified plug-ins loaded. The next time you restart Acrobat, only certified plug-ins are loaded.

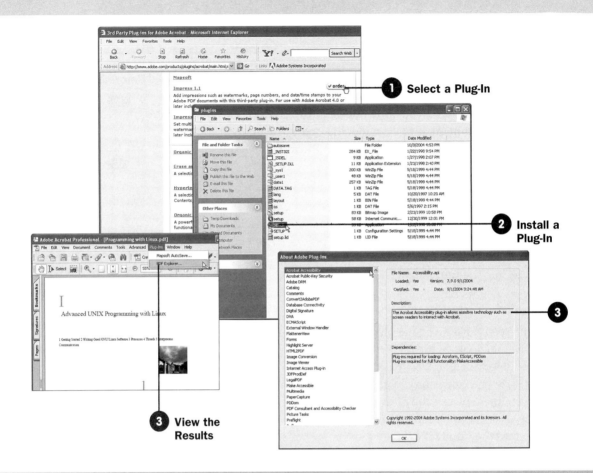

1 Select a Plug-In

2 Install a Plug-In

3 View the Results

 TIP

To unzip zipped files, you need a file extractor. For Windows users, a free evaluation version of WinZip is available at http://www.winzip.com. Mac OS users can use the operating system's built-in decompression feature or can download StuffIt Expander from http://www.stuffit.com.

If you are not sure what a plug-in does or where it came from, view the plug-in's information found under the **Help** menu—select **About Third-Party Plug-Ins** and select the plug-in. A dialog box appears with information on the plug-in, such as the copyright information and a website to visit for more information.

You can also view Acrobat plug-ins by going to the **Help** menu and selecting the **About Adobe Plug-Ins** command. The **About Adobe Plug-Ins** dialog box appears. On the left side of the dialog box is a list of all the Adobe plug-ins, and on the right side is the plug-in information. Select a plug-in to view the version, whether it is certified, the creation date, a description of what the plug-in does, and its dependencies.

83 About Sources for Plug-Ins

If you have specific functionality that you need but that Acrobat does not provide, a third-party plug-in solution is probably available on the Web. Most plug-ins must be purchased before downloading them. However, some websites allow you to download a trial version of the plug-in that either has limited functionality or expires after a set number of days.

A huge assortment of plug-ins is available for Acrobat. For a broad selection of popular plug-ins from various developers, we recommend visiting the Acrobat plug-in page of the official Adobe website at http://store.adobe.com/store/products/plugins/. Other good sources for Acrobat plug-ins and information include the PDF Store (http://www.pdfstore.com); Planet PDF (http://www.planetpdf.com/); The World-Wide Power Company, LLC (http://www.thepowerco.com/); and PluginsWorld (http://pluginsworld.com). On each of these sites, you can find plug-ins from many manufacturers.

For example, The World-Wide Power Company, LLC offers an auto-save plug-in that automatically saves your PDF as you're working. PluginsWorld offers a plug-in that enables you to erase content from your PDF.

Index

A

B

background color, 112

Background Removal option (Image Settings dialog box), 196

bleeds, 38

Bookmark tab (Acrobat PDFMaker dialog box), 29

bookmarks

    changing, 120-121

    creating in the same document, 118-120

    creating to different documents, 122-124

    definition of, 118

    deleting, 120

    generating from structured documents, 125-127

    naming, 120

    nesting, 129

    organizing, 127-129

    rearranging, 129

    renaming, 120, 127

    structured bookmarks, 125

Bookmarks panel, 15

books, digital. *See* digital editions

Border palette (Adobe Designer), 136

borrowing digital editions, 162

Braille, printing documents in, 168

Browse for Folder dialog box, 36

browser-based reviews

    definition of, 50

    review process, 54-56

Button Properties dialog box, 103, 154-155

Button tool, 103-105

buttons

    creating, 103-105

    editing, 106

    properties, 103, 154-155

    radio buttons

        adding to PDF forms, 143, 152

        exclusive groups, 143

C

certified plug-ins, 211

certifying PDF files, 90-92

CGI applications, 153

Change Conversion Settings command (Adobe PDF menu), 27, 108

Changes Allowed permissions, 83-84

changing PDFs. *See* modifying PDFs

Check Box Properties dialog box, 152

Check Box tool, 143, 152

check boxes, adding to PDF forms, 143, 152

Check for New Issues command (My Digital Editions window), 165

choosing passwords, 82

Clip Complex Regions option (Raster/Vector Balance dialog box), 190

collapsing nested bookmarks, 129

color

    color output, previewing, 179-180

    presentation background color, 112

D

How can we make this index more useful? Email us at indexes@samspublishing.com

219

E

F

How can we make this index more useful? Email us at indexes@samspublishing.com

221

G-H

I

How can we make this index more useful? Email us at indexes@samspublishing.com

223

How can we make this index more useful? Email us at indexes@samspublishing.com

225

How can we make this index more useful? Email us at indexes@samspublishing.com

227

R

How can we make this index more useful? Email us at indexes@samspublishing.com

229

security

T

tags, 125

Task toolbar

    Convert to Adobe PDF button, 29

    Create PDF button, 21

templates, 23

    editing, 146

    form templates, 144-146

testing multimedia links, 111

text

    comments, 63-64

    converting scanned documents to, 197-198

    editing, 45-47

    text fields, adding to PDF forms, 141-142, 149, 152

Text Edits menu commands, Indicate Text Edits Tool, 63

Text Field Properties dialog box, 149

Text Integration Summary dialog box, 72

third-party plug-ins

    certified, 211

    definition of, 210

    disabling, 210

    how they work, 210

    installing, 211-212

    non-certified, 211

    plug_ins folder, 210

    sources for, 213

toolbar well, 12

toolbars. *See names of specific toolbars*

tools

    Button, 103-105

    Check Box, 143, 152

    Combo Box, 152

    Crop, 38

    Drop-Down List, 144

    hidden tools, accessing, 12

    Link

        menu action links, 101-102

        multimedia links, 96-98

        navigation links, 99

    List, 152

    Movie, 110

    Note, 59

    Radio Button, 143, 152

    Sound, 110

    Stamp, 62

    TouchUp Text Tool, 45

    Zoom, 13

TouchUp Properties dialog box, 47

TouchUp Text Tool, 45

Tracker, 56-58

transitions, 113-115

transparency flattening, 189-190

trapping, 178-179

U

unzipping files, 212

Upload for Browser-Based Review command (Send for Review menu), 54

user interface (Acrobat), 11

    Comments pane, 15-16

    Document pane, 13-15

    How To pane, 16

    Navigation pane, 15

    toolbar well, 12

    toolbars, 12-13

users with disabilities. *See accessibility*

Key Terms

Don't let unfamiliar terms discourage you from learning all you can about Adobe Acrobat. If you don't completely understand what one of these words means, flip to the indicated page, read the full definition there, and find techniques related to that term.

Accessibility
When used to refer to PDF files, means document accessibility for vision- or motion-impaired users.
Page 168

Actions
In Acrobat they include displaying specific document location, executing menu commands, playing multimedia files, running JavaScript, and so on. The term specifically refers to such actions taken in response to user input, such as clicking a button. **94**

Bookmark
A special type of navigation link that appears in the Bookmarks panel of the navigation pane, rather than in the document itself. **118**

Browser-based reviews
A review process where the PDF is stored in one location, usually on a shared server, and accessed by the reviewers via a web browser. **50**

CGI (Common Gateway Interface) applications
Small applications that run on web servers. They perform a variety of tasks, including accepting incoming data and storing it in database form. **153**

Cropping
The process of trimming away unwanted areas around the perimeter of a page or a selected portion of a page. **32**

Digital editions
Books in digital format which can be displayed on a computer or handheld device. **158**

Digital signature
A unique digital identifier that allows a user to certify that a document has been created, reviewed, or approved. Digital signatures are used in much the same way that handwritten signatures are used. **6**

Dynamic forms
A type of interactive form that adjusts to the amount of content to be displayed and how much information is entered by the end user. **135**

eBook
The traditional term for digital editions. **158**

eEnvelope
An unencrypted PDF file that contains encrypted attachments. **91**

Email-based reviews
A review process where PDFs are sent by email as an attachment to recipients for commenting. **50**

Embedded fonts
Fonts whose information is stored within the PDF file itself. This ensures that the fonts will display and print correctly even if the user does not have the fonts installed on his computer. **Page 45**

Exclusive groups
Groups of radio buttons among which only one button can be active at a time. A common example would be a multiple choice questionnaire. Each question would have an exclusive group of responses, among which the user can choose only one. **143**

Extracting
When executed on a page or range of pages, it creates a new PDF file that contains those pages. The selected page or pages may be deleted from the original document, if desired, during the process. **34**

Footer
Text or images that appear at the bottom of a range of printed pages. **43**

Form elements
Refers to all the objects on a form that allow user input, such as text boxes, radio buttons, check boxes, drop-down lists, and so on. **134**

Header
Text or images that appear at the top of a range of printed pages. **43**

HTML
Stands for Hypertext Markup Language, a language used to define how text and images are displayed on the Web. **134**

Interactive forms
Forms that allow end users to enter data directly into a form and have it electronically delivered either by email or to a database. **135**

Job options
The term used in previous versions of Distiller for default settings. These settings files still use the .joboptions suffix. **204**

Links
In Acrobat they are clickable areas that perform an action. The most common types of links are navigation links, which take you to a new location, but links can also run JavaScript, execute menu items, play sounds or video, and so on. **94**

Misregistration
The result of poorly aligned printing passes, it results in unwanted gaps or between colors. **178**